This book contains 129 messages that John Ed Mathison has written to the Frazer family on the front of the weekly bulletin of the Frazer Memorial United Methodist Church. He has made it a practice to utilize the front page of the bulletin each week to share with the Frazer family. Many of these lessons of life are taken from the experiences within his life and the life of the church.

After the title message, "Fishing for Birds," the messages are listed chronologically beginning with January 13, 1974. The date of each bulletin message is listed at the bottom of the page.

John Crawford, a member of the Frazer family and the political cartoonist for the *Montgomery Advertiser-Journal*, illustrated the cover.

The purpose of these messages is to convict, motivate, and encourage us to follow the plan and purpose that Jesus Christ has for us as individuals and as a church. The individual lessons might be used as a daily devotional guide, and the book as a whole will give the reader some sense of the growth of the church and the flavor of its family life.

FISHING FOR BIRDS

My five-year old son asked me several times last fall to take him fishing, but we never got around to it. So for Christmas I found a present from him which was one half inch thick and six feet long. Also under the tree was a small package which was a jar of live worms!

Well, we still haven't been fishing yet, so he decided recently to use his own creative genius. I came home one day and found him standing in the middle of the backyard — fishing pole, line, worms and all. I asked him what he was doing, and he said, "Trying to catch some birds." I tried to explain that's not the way to catch birds, but he quickly said, "Fish like worms, and you catch them on a hook. Birds like worms too, so I'll catch some birds until we go fishing."

I didn't have an answer to that. It sounded logical and reasonable, except that it doesn't work that way. Then I thought how often I select a way to do something that seems logical and reasonable to me, but it doesn't work out because it's not God's way. Then I thought of the verses which say, "there is a way that seems right to man, but the end is destruction"; "the way of a fool is right in his own eyes"; "your ways are not my ways, says the Lord."

Easter faith is a faith of doing things God's way. After all, the crucifixion and resurrection defied human logic — but it was God's way.

On the first Sunday after Easter, I challenge us to look at our values to see if things that seem so logical and reasonable to us look the same to God. We might be fishing for birds.

See you at the "fishing" place Sunday!

— John Ed

April 6, 1975

PEDAL POWER

My young friend Mike Wallace received a nice visit from Santa which included a two-seater bicycle. He came by my house to show it to me and give me a lesson in riding it. I've ridden a regular bicycle, and even a 10-speed, but this was different.

Mike put me on the front seat and he got on the back. We rode a little way and I thought I was getting tired awfully fast and the bike was getting harder to pedal. Then I heard Mike laughing and discovered that he had quit pedaling and was just sitting there. I was doing all the pedaling. I thought about the church — a lot of us would like to take the back seat and "just coast" while somebody else is doing the work. We know that we ought to "do our share", but its easier to sit back and relax and look and enjoy the ride at the expense of somebody else's work.

Mike told me that one reason folks prefer the front seat to the back is that the guy on the back can pedal but doesn't get to guide. Only the guy on the front seat holds the handle bars that determine the direction of the bike. Mike jokingly said he always puts the girls on the back because they can't make up their minds which way to go! Again I thought how in the church we don't mind pedaling as long as we're guiding, but we don't want to pedal if someone else is making the decisions. Also we better not try putting the women on the back seat because they often make better and quicker decisions than the men.

One thing I found out about the two-seater is that it will really travel when both people are pedaling together. The same is true of the church.

Pick a place and let's pedal!

— *John Ed*

January 13, 1974

SPARE THE PAPER — SPOIL THE PERSON

I wouldn't have believed it unless I had seen it. And I saw it. A friend of mine had a small fruit tree that had done nothing since it was planted — no leaves or buds. A friend who studies plants and gives lectures to gardeners offered a strange suggestion to my friend. He was told the tree needed a spanking. That's right — a spanking.

So my friend selected a time when no neighbors were home. After all, they know him as a stable person. He rolled up some newspapers and went to his tree. I'm sure he said to the tree, "This is going to hurt me worse than you," and proceeded to spank it. Would you believe (and I saw it with my own eyes) that it now has leaves and buds. It is producing. The only explanation my friend can give is that the spanking disturbed the roots and caused the plant to start growing.

Maybe a lot of us need disturbing — or spanking. I'm sure God would like to see our lives producing more fruit and beauty. I'm sure all of us have hidden lots of talents that need to be activated. I know it is easy for us to become content with the way things are.

It is easy for our nation to become complacent. As a nation we need to be disturbed. We need to think God's thoughts. We need to produce the kind of fruit He values.

Remember the fig tree in Luke 13. There was nothing wrong with it except that it was failing to produce figs.

I would like to ask God to "roll up His paper" and disturb me and my church and my nation where we need it.

— John Ed

July 7, 1974

HE MISSED HIS BIG MOMENT

Last week I was invited to speak at the awards banquet for the National League of the Dixie Youth baseball. The climax of the program came when the awards were to be made to the all-stars from the various teams.

Here was the Mayor, the City Commissioners, and the State President of Dixie Youth ready to present the awards. Here were the boys on the teams, their parents, their coaches, and their sponsors. The first name (I'll say John Doe) was read. The people applauded, but John Doe didn't step forward. The master of ceremonies asked if he was present and several boys said yes. He called his name again. After a brief silence a voice in the back of the room sheepishly said, "He's gone to the bathroom."

His big moment — and he was in the bathroom. I know some of you are thinking that if the speech hadn't been so long, John wouldn't have been out.

I wonder how often God calls our name for some reason — and there is no answer. Maybe there is something He wants us to do or something He wants to teach us or show us, and we are unavailable. How many times in life have big moments come, and we were "in the bathroom."

Be ready — God might be announcing you for a special team at any time!

— John Ed

July 14, 1974

KEEP YOUR FEET MOVING

Last week I was watching the men pour the slab for the Sanctuary. It is four inches thick. The concrete came sliding down the chute from the mixer. Three or four men in high boots got in the middle of it and started spreading it. They worked fast. The foreman said to me, "When you're standing in that wet cement, you don't stay long in the same place."

I could see what he was talking about. If you stayed long enough in one place for it to set up, you would be there.

The Christian faith is something like this. It is growth — movement in the right direction. If you stay in one place in your faith for long, you become dull, stale, and eventually dead — no excitement, joy, or growth.

The faith doesn't keep us out of the "cement" of life like jealousy, selfishness, gossip, fault-finding, resentment, temptation, judging, over-indulgence, etc. We aren't shielded from these — we have to walk around in them everyday. But if we stay very long in one place with any of the "sins that so easily beset us," we'll be trapped there.

When the men spread the concrete, got out of it, and leveled it, it made a solid foundation for the new church building. Let's don't stay where we are — new ideas, commitments, converts, visits, witness, challenges, dreams, insights will get us out of the things that would "lock us in" and free us to be the foundation for the church He's building.

I'm picking up my feet . . . .!

— *John Ed*

July 21, 1974

5

EXPLETIVE DELETED

Since Watergate, the government now has hired 247 tape listeners to replace dirty words on tapes with "expletives deleted." One man can listen to eight miles of tape in a 40 hour week. His rating is GS6 and he earns $9,000 a year. He estimates that he has heard about 3 million dirty words in the past 2 years.

Maybe we need to listen to some of our conversations (tapes) and see if we ought to erase some things with "expletive deleted." I'm not thinking just of four letter (or however many letters it takes to spell them) words, but conversations involving gossip, judgement of others, sharing confidences about others, etc. After all, Webster defines profanity as "to violate or treat with irreverance; to desecrate." Desecrating or violating another personality might be more serious than four letter words.

Let's try checking out our conversations about others. How much would be erased with "expletive deleted?" We might tend to be like the person who said, "You can't believe everything you hear, but you can repeat it." Or like the lady in the beauty parlor who said the talk alone was enough to curl her hair. And the telephone — when it comes to picking up dirt the vacuum cleaner can't compare with the telephone. Of course we men don't gossip — we just repeat rumors we've heard but don't believe.

Well, this is the beginning of the sermon for Sunday. I can't offer us a GS6 to listen to our tapes, but I have a better suggestion. And it's guaranteed. It won't cost $9,000 — it's free; but it may cost us all a lot of conversation in the long run!

— John Ed

August 11, 1974

SITTING ON THE SIDE OF THE POOL

I went down to the Y.M.C.A. on a Friday night recently with my family to go swimming. I was sitting on the edge of the pool watching the kids swim when I noticed a little fellow, about five years old, enter the pool area. He was ready to swim. He had on a fancy bathing suit, swim fins, diving mask, snorkle tube, and I don't know what else. He looked like he had as much equipment as a professional scuba diver.

Well, the little fellow sat on the side of the pool. He watched everybody swim. He never got in the water. He just kicked it a little with his feet. He had all the necessary equipment at his disposal for an exciting swim, but he was contented to dangle his feet in the water.

I saw myself and the church in that little fellow. God has placed at our disposal all the necessary ingredients for life to be an exciting adventure. The church is standing on the threshold of her finest hour. God is calling us to launch out into new and creative roles of witness and service. God wants us to experience a fun in the faith that is like a refreshing swim. But too often we are just contented to sit on the side and watch.

I wondered when the little fellow would get up the courage to get in the pool and use what he had. He will sometime, and what fun he will have! And the same is true for any of us . . .

— John Ed

August 18, 1974

95,000 BRICKS

About 6 weeks ago several loads of bricks were delivered for the new building. They were unloaded in different places in the church yard. When I inquired as to how many bricks would be used, the foreman replied, "95,000."

Well, last week they started taking these bricks from the stacks and building the walls of the new building. For several weeks they did nothing except occupy space (and eliminate some of the grass area that Larry Westfall had to cut). Now some skilled men are putting them together to build a church building.

Sometimes God must think that we are like those bricks, just sitting and occupying space — not doing much harm, but doing no good. Like the bricks, we were created for a purpose, and God's greatest desire for us is that we place our lives into His skilled hands so that He might put us in our proper place.

I wonder what the building would be like if some of the bricks refused to be used, or decided to "drop out." It would mar the beauty of the building, and the "spaces" would make heating and cooling awfully difficult. Any of us members who are not fulfilling our proper place mar the ministry of the Church in much the same manner.

What if some bricks didn't carry their share of the load? The walls would be weak and the building would not be safe. I challenge us to evaluate and see if we are "carrying our share" in the Church through our prayers, presence, gifts, and service. Are we a part of the strength or weakness of the Church?

As the walls go up you notice the individual bricks, and see the unit as a whole. As Frazer grows, I hope the same is true.

Each brick is important . . . and so are you. Let's build!

— *John Ed*

September 8, 1974

A LITTLE LADY LEARNS A BIG LESSON

When our family received our letter 2 weeks ago from the finance committee thanking us for our giving and indicating our record of giving for the first quarter of the church year, my eight-year old daughter and I were looking at it. There was a record of her giving also, and it wasn't consistent with what she had said she would give. She had missed some Sundays.

When I asked about it, she replied that she just hadn't been able to give each Sunday. She explained that she had been to TG&Y and bought some things for school and some other things she wanted. Then she asked, "What do you do when you don't have any money left for church?"

Well, fortunately our family giving was current with what we had estimated. I showed her our slip. I told her that the first check Joan and I write when we get paid is the check to the Church. It is 10% of what the Church pays us. We write that check first, and then we look at the other places we will spend our money. I explained that when you put first things first, other things will fall in their proper place.

I don't always set the best example for my kids, but I'm glad I did in this area. I'm glad I grew up in a family that set it for me — they didn't 'talk' Christianity but "did" it. Any person who talks about loving the church and God and isn't living it through the area of giving — the words have an empty ring.

Vicki looked at me and smiled and said, "Then it's important what you spend first, isn't it?" I think she had learned a big lesson — and I had relearned it.

— *John Ed*

September 15, 1974

TALKING WITHOUT WORDS

Our week-day kindergarten enrolled a little five-year old boy from Guatemala. He speaks no English. It would have been easier not to accept him since he would require more time, but the teachers accepted him not as a problem but an opportunity.

Well, Smokey the Bear came to school last week during Fire Prevention Week. He danced a little for the kids and then allowed them to ask questions. After a couple of the kids asked questions, Fernado's hand went up. When Smokey recognized him, Fernado came up to him and shook his hand. No words were exchanged, but the excited look on Fernado's face communicated more than words could describe.

I've observed Fernado with the other kids. He is learning some English, but he and the kids don't really need words to communicate. Through gestures, expressions, pictures, etc., they communicate with each other. The other day Fernado came out with an expression he had heard, "Come on." One of his buddies was so excited that he ran over to Fernado and gave him a big bear hug. No words, but genuine communication.

Most of our communication isn't with words. One study determined that only 20% of daily communication is with words. Our facial expressions, gestures, appearance, etc. send more messages than our lips. If we are "communicators of the Good News," then we are at all times so loud people don't hear what we say.

Also I remember how frightened Fernado was the first day he came. He was crying and didn't want to stay with all those strange people. However, the kids and teachers communicated (without words) love and acceptance and joy, and now Fernado is a part of the group and loves it. There's a lesson here for us as we have new people at church every Sunday and meet new people every day.

Every person we meet is receiving *some* message from us . . .

— *John Ed*

October 20, 1974

10

WHO WON THE GAME

My third grade daughter Vicki has really been excited this Fall because she signed up for cheerleader for the Dozier Cub team. The cheerleaders take their work seriously. They practice two days a week — and numerous hours at home. Vicki had learned twenty-one cheers. The cheers have become so much a part of her current life-style that recently she bowed her head at a meal and instead of praying just automatically started one of the cheers.

I remember going to her first game a few weeks ago. Mother had spent hours on her uniform. The whole game the cheerleaders went through their cheers. They cheered with enthusiasm and intense feeling. They had all the cheers and motions coordinated. They acted as if they were pulling for a national championship team. As we were leaving the field after the game, Vicki, who was almost exhausted, said she needed to ask me something. I leaned over and she said, "Daddy, who won the game?"

She had no idea how to keep score. She was just doing the cheers and acting like cheerleaders she had seen on T.V. She was having fun — but it centered on what she was doing. Think of the fun she will have when she sees what she is doing in relation to its purpose — to the team, the game, the student body, etc.

I wonder how many of us who go through church knowing all the songs, and the prayers, and the creeds, and acting like people we've seen, but never knowing what its' all about. We know the words, but have never experienced the meaning. As James writes, we have the *form* but lack the *power* of faith.

Don't be guilty of just "cheering" at church, then waking up someday and asking "who won the game".

— *John Ed*

November 3, 1974

11

PREDICTING-PRONOUNCING-PROPHESYING

I had a lot of fun last week when I was invited to be the "grid guesspert" by the sportswriters for the Alabama Journal and pick the football winners for the weekend. One of them complained because he said I was supposed to be a "prophet".

There is a very popular misunderstanding about the meaning of prophet. Most folks think of a prophet as one who predicts the future. The Biblical understanding of a prophet is not a "predicter of the future but a "proclaimer of God's Word." The emphasis is not on the future, but on faithfulness to God's Word.

I think this is so important today because of the widespread interest in astrology and people who are writing about Biblical predictions. No one — no one but God knows the future. It's fascinating and interesting, and people will pay money to read or hear about what is going to happen, but don't fall for it! Heed Jesus' warning to the people of His day that "you do not know the day nor the hour . . ." Be a responsible steward of the responsibility assigned you now, and the future will take care of itself. The dates and times and fact are in His domain.

People like to hear predictions — prophets have never fared well. When the preacher pronounces God's Word about the use of our money and time and talent and priorities — we like to change the subject.

I didn't do too badly predicting — I got 14 out of 20, which is about the season average of the writers. If Auburn, Georgia, Georgia Tech, and Mississippi State had . . . well, never mind.

I'd rather have a good record as a prophet — and He is helping me work on that!

— John Ed

November 10, 1974

12

WRONG SHOE ON THE RIGHT FOOT

Sunday mornings around the parsonage might be a little different from your house because I get up early and leave before 8:00 and that means Joan has to get the kids ready by herself. It is especially frantic for her on the 4th Sundays because she keeps the nursery at 11:00, so she attends the 8:40 service.

So, on a 4th Sunday recently she enlisted the help of Vicki, our eight-year old, in getting Si, five years old, dressed for church. Now Si has never been too fond of Sunday shoes, tie, and coat, but his big sister hurriedly helped him. During Church School I went down to his class and he was complaining about those Sunday shoes. At about the same time his teacher and I looked at his feet and discovered the problem —Vicki had put his right shoe on his left foot and vice versa.

No wonder his feet were hurting. No wonder walking was a little complicated. No wonder he had a whinning attitude and life was miserable for him, and he was making it miserable for everybody else. No wonder he didn't like Church School. No wonder he resisted encouragement to be a "good boy".

Whenever we get the wrong priorities in life and give significant value to insignificant items and vice versa, life feels pinched and painful, and happy living becomes complicated. We feel miserable and make others miserable. Ninety-nine percent of what we feel is wrong with the church and others is really what is wrong with us because our "feet" are hurting so much because we have the wrong shoes on the wrong foot.

At the beginning of this year, I challenge us to evaluate our priorities. How are we spending our time — our money — our energy. Do we have the right shoes on the right feet!

When I told Vicki she had put the wrong shoe on the right foot, she quickly corrected me to say she had the right shoe, but the wrong foot. Either way, it still hurt Si. Defensive rationalizing didn't heal the hurt. Changing the shoes did.

It's not too late for some shoe changing . . .!

— *John Ed*

January 5, 1975

13

THE UNANSWERABLE ARGUMENT

I was at a meeting at the Y.M.C.A. last week when I overheard a man telling about a certain diet. When he started describing all the things you could eat, and the portions you could eat on this diet, he was interrupted by several fellows who said the diet wouldn't work. They argued back and forth for fifteen minutes. One man was even giving "physiological evidence" of why the diet wouldn't work. The group about had me convinced that the man was wrong until a doctor stepped in and said, "I have the records to show that this man started the diet seven months ago and has lost thirty pounds. He's proof that it works."

That ended the argument. The reality of one person's experience negated all the "reasoning" of the group. You can always argue about things you think ought reasonably to be a certain way, but living proof is the argument for which there is no reply.

I believe the greatest task of the church today is to quit arguing its case verbally and demonstrate what the church is about with changed lives. You can present sociological and psychological data that reasonably convinces that human nature doesn't radically change, but one person who has found new life is an unanswerable argument for the fact that God in Christ does change lives. You can argue with philosophies, but a changed life is as evident as lost weight.

Read Paul's journey in Acts. At different places people would begin debating with him and he would reply, "One day I was going to Damascus . . ." And the difference in Saul and Paul before and after that trip to Damascus was proof of what God could do. His personal experience was his strongest argument.

Are our lives arguments for or against what the church is all about?

— *John Ed*

January 19, 1978

BURDENS OR BLESSINGS

A little boy named Ricky Ray lives in our area. He is physically handicapped with spastic cerebral palsy. He is basically confined to a wheelchair and thereby dependent on others. Both legs and one arm are seriously afflicted.

When Ricky's parents requested application to some kindergartens in town, they were turned down because of the individual time and attention he required. The teachers in our kindergarten decided to accept him.

Rather than a burden, Ricky has turned out to be a blessing. The kids love him. They have to take turns to push him to play, to the bathroom, etc. They genuinely look after him. While Ricky has a physical handicap, he has been abundantly blessed with a good sense of humor, a delightful disposition, and a good mind. Everyone around him is blessed by his presence.

The kids really pull for him. One morning I heard excitement in the hall, and the kids had lined the wall, with looks of amazement on their faces. At the end of the hall was Ricky with a walker instead of a wheelchair. He was taking a few steps. The children started clapping. They ran up to him to congratulate him. I think Ricky was as proud as Neil Armstrong when he put his foot on the moon.

Ricky has been a blessing to me. His radiant smile and appreciative spirit are an inspiration. I'm glad our kindergarten cared enough to take him. They've found that the kids have helped him so much, and Ricky has taught them so much that he has been a blessing rather than a burden.

God has a way of turning burdens into blessings!

— *John Ed*

April 20, 1975

15

THE DAY BEFORE TOMORROW

My son, Si, and a neighbor, Jason Slatton, ride with me each morning to the church for kindergarten. They are in the 4 year class. I've received an education by just listening to them each day. Last fall they discovered they had the same birthday. One of them exclaimed, "Hey, we're twins — we just got different mothers."

Recently, Si was trying to reform Jason of an annoying habit. Jason refused to change. Finally, after the long persistence of Si, Jason said he would change. Si asked him when he would change, and he replied, "the day before tomorrow."

Of course he got his words mixed up, but he came out with a pretty good statement about the time for improvement. It sounds to me like "the day before tomorrow" is now. And that is a pretty good time to make some changes that we so easily put off. Jesus taught that the Kingdom of God is now ... He called people to repent and live *now* ... He invited people to be disciples *now* .... He offered the abundant life *now* ....

I have a feeling that many of us are struggling with decisions and changes we ought to make, but are going to do it the "day after tomorrow" (which is probably never). Maybe you ought to volunteer now to teach Sunday School, to serve as a visitor or an usher, to tithe, to rearrange priorities, to change some bad habits.

The best time to begin the kind of life God wants us to live is the day before tomorrow!

— John Ed

May 18, 1978

RECEIVING AND GIVING

About twelve years ago, a young minister was enjoying a tremendous ministry here in Montgomery. He was a part of a young, growing, dynamic congregation. His witness touched the lives of many people, but one person in a special way. That person became very active in the church and was a real leader. He quickly attributes much of his growth in the Christian faith and involvement in the church to that young minister.

The minister moved a few years later, and eventually went to work with the government agency O.E.O. He started developing headaches, and doctors discovered he had a brain tumor. There was a lengthy surgical procedure, and subsequent surgeries. Several times the young man almost died. For over a year he lay immobile in a bed, and then a couple of years in a convalescent home. He couldn't walk or talk. His wife divorced him. His mother and father died. He was very depressed and despondent. The future looked bleak to him.

One person, among many others, who never gave up on him was that layman in Montgomery. Their roles were completely switched now as the layman "ministered" to him. He made trips to Atlanta. He encouraged him. As the young minister made progress, the layman brought him to Montgomery for visits.

That layman is Robert Gardner and he is now a member of Frazer. His daughter was married in our sanctuary last Saturday, and that minister, O.C. Brown, "stood" with me and placed his hands on that couple's heads for the marriage blessing. He still can't talk, and someone has to help him walk, but he has made 100% progress in recent months. His progress has been aided by lots of lay folks who are ministering to him (and he still has a great ministry to them).

He graphically reminded me of how much we need each other. We might be on the receiving or giving end now, but the roles could quickly be reversed. No one is so strong that he doesn't need to receive, nor so weak that he can't give. Somebody needs what you have to give.

Giving and receiving is what Christian living is all about!

— *John Ed*

June 15, 1975

READ THE DIRECTIONS FIRST

The parsonage has a fenced backyard. One of the problems in mowing the lawn is cutting the grass next to the fence. Last year I came up with a bright idea. Bill Baldwin had given the Church some poison to kill weeds. I borrowed the tank compressor and the poison and figured I would put a little along the edge of the fence and that would take care of that grass that was so difficult to get to. I even decided to put a little along the edge of the sidewalk so I wouldn't have to edge it. I was ready to start writing my speech to accept the Yard of The Month Award!

One thing I failed to do—read the directions. I wanted to kill the grass quickly so I didn't dilute the poison in the right proportions. I figured a little extra poison would kill the grass extra fast. Well, when it rained that poison started spreading underground. It killed the grass around the fence all right, and in a couple of weeks started on my neighbor's yard — first a couple of feet and then 8 to 10 feet into his yard. It killed everything. He was very nice, but I was expecting a call from his lawyer. It spread to our one little tree in the backyard, and it died. I had a one foot border down each side of the sidewalk. My great idea was a tragedy.

I never intended to ruin my yard or my neighbors. I just didn't read the directions. And most of us in life don't intend to make a mess of our lives, or hurt our neighbors. But so often we try to prescribe life according to our "reasoning" rather than reading the directions from Him who created life.

The Bible contains all the ingredients and the proper proportions for the most beautiful life possible. I hope you learn the lesson I learned — read the directions first, then follow them.

See you at the "directions" place Sunday!

— *John Ed*

July 27, 1975

WHAT DOES THE SIGN SAY?

Our children recently spent a week with their grandparents in Panama City. One of the things that impressed my five-year old son most was a Holiday Inn billboard there with the message — "We can't spell success without "U". Obviously, someone read the billboard to him and quickly he picked up the message and began repeating it. Now *everytime* he sees a Holiday Inn sign he quotes the message — "We can't spell success without U". It doesn't matter what the particular sign says, he contends that the same message is there.

Being unable to read, he learned the message by association with the sign rather than what the sign actually said. It seems to me that this is a very important concept that all of us adults and parents ought to remember in the church. Our kids do not learn so much from us by what we say but by the association of the things we do. The lessons we teach them most are not the lectures we give to them, but how we act in the different circumstances of life.

And I feel that this is the greatest demand the world is making on the church today. The world isn't so interested in theology and sermons, but it is vitally interested in seeing the results of meaningful living by real people. What our lips are saying is not nearly so important to the man of the world, as what he associates our attitude and disposition and general outlook as expressed in our living.

In the movie, "My Fair Lady", there is a song called "Show Me" which says, "Words, words, words. I'm sick of words. Sing me no songs, read me no rhymes, don't waste my time, Show me." Jesus put it this way when He said, "Not everyone who says Lord, Lord, shall enter the kingdom, But he who *does* My will."

More people are convinced about Christianity by the association of actions than they are by the wisdom of words. Our signs are saying something to somebody!

— *John Ed*

August 10, 1975

DRAFTING IS THE KEY

A former winner of the Talladega 500, Dick Brooks, was quoted last week as saying, "The key to winning the Talladega 500 is drafting." He then predicted that at the opening gun there would be a mad scramble to get in the draft and that nobody would want to lead the race until the checkered flag.

Since I have never been to a big race, this was unfamiliar to me. So I asked Frazer's Resident Racing Expert, Bill Westfall, about it. He explained that the Talladega 500 racetrack is a banked track. This means that the cars can run wide open for the whole race. When one car gets right on the bumper of another car at a high rate of speed, this creates a draft. This makes both cars go faster. For this reason, drivers will team up with each other to get in the draft. Westfall further explained that the race is too long for one car to run it wide open by itself.

While I don't know anything about car racing, I know enough about life to know that the principle of drafting is essential to living, too. Nobody is capable of holding up throughout life by himself. Life takes on meaning when people team up together. Each of us needs each other. Each person has something unique to contribute to the life of another person.

The young people have a song which talks about being down and out, troubled, and needing somebody, and then says, "You just call out my name and you know wherever I am, I'll come running to see you again. Winter, Spring, Summer or Fall, All you have to do is call, And I'll be there, You've got a friend."

Frazer is a great place for drafting! People are finding that this is the key. The leaders at the checkered flag of life will be those who get into the draft early.

Tim and Phillip will be preaching in my absence at the "drafting place" Sunday. Team up with some folks and get into the draft!

— *John Ed*

August 24, 1975

TWO ROOFS ARE BETTER THAN ONE

Several people have been inquiring about the shingles in front of the church and the new roofing being placed on the new sanctuary. Everybody wanted to know if the roof was leaking. Actually, there was a slight imperfection in the coloring of some of the shingles and the roofing did not pass the inspection. So the contractor just placed a new roof over the 4-month old roof. Both roofs carry a 20 year guarantee so we shouldn't have a leak for a long time.

It was very important that every phase of the new building measure up to the standards. With this correction in the roofing most of the building meets the standards. A good question for all of us to ask might be, "How well does the real church (the people) measure up to the standards set for it?" It might be that all of us need to take a new look at ourselves and see if we measure up to the standards of churchmanship. We might find some imperfect coloring and malfunctions in our life-style. But the Builder can correct that, and make us twice as strong as before.

The new building is fulfilling a vital function in providing for our worshipping community a place to celebrate worship each week. It is fulfilling its function. The real task before us is for the real church to fulfill its function as we become the "salt of the earth and the light of the world."

Oh! If you have any friends that said that they couldn't come to church because the roof might fall in, you might tell them that our church has a double roof so they would be safe to come!

See you at the inspection passing place Sunday!

— *John Ed*

September 21, 1975

WHAT HAPPENED TO THE TREES

Last week I, along with five other ministers from Montgomery, went down to the First United Methodist Church of Ft. Walton Beach for a We Care Mission. Both of the ministers from that church had participated in our We Care Mission.

This was the week following hurricane Eloise. Several of us wondered if they would even still have the Mission and I think all of us were curious about the amount of damage done to Ft. Walton Beach.

One of the things that surprised me about the hurricane damage was to see several areas of thickly populated trees. The strange thing was that in an area with so many trees only a few of them were uprooted. There were other trees all around them that were seemingly untouched by the winds. I casually commented to a friend how this could happen. He quickly replied that the trees that are still standing had roots deep enough to hold the whole tree steady during the strong winds. The trees that fell had very shallow roots that were insufficient to hold them in the ground. Someone also said that the trees that withstood the storms became stronger because the demands made on the roots will cause them to grow more.

I thought how much life is like this. Many people face the same kind of situations in life and some fold and others become stronger. I think the secret is the depth of the roots of our faith and our commitment When the storms of life blow hard, people whose roots of faith and commitment run shallow are quickly blown over — others seem to be strengthened.

The fellowship of the church and the disciplines of faith are the best means I know of strengthening our roots of commitment. And roots really grow in the rain (for trees and people) — like the huge attendance and participation we had on a rainy day last Sunday.

See you at the "root-developing" place Sunday!

— John Ed

October 12, 1975

CONTROLLED FLIGHT

Bob and Doris Rich of Chicago recently landed their radio-controlled, Liberty Bell, model airplane at the TG&Y Shopping center. Tim and I heard about it and went down to see it land.

Montgomery is one of the 14 major cities at which the aircraft will stop enroute from Kitty Hawk, North Carolina to the west coast. While in flight the six-foot wing span Liberty Bell is controlled from the back of a pick-up truck. The Rich's are attempting to set a transcontinental record for radio-controlled flight in commemoration of the Bicentennial.

One of our members, Carl Russell, flies model planes as a hobby. He was explaining to Tim and me some of the fascinating aspects of flying model airplanes. He insisted that the man with the radio controls the flight of the plane. The plane simply responds to his signals and performs as he directs.

Carl made one interesting observation — he said that sometimes a CB radio might be on the same channel as the radio operating the plane. When this happens, problems can occur. The plane doesn't know which radio signals to react to and the CB radio channel can actually cause the plane to crash or to get beyond the radio signals of the original receiver.

I have a feeling that our lives function best when they are controlled completely by Him who created us. Our problems occur when we tune in to "signals" from other channels and become confused about which pattern to follow. Immense problems are the end result.

Commemoration of the Bicentennial is a good time to start a new record for God-controlled living.

See you at the channel that sends the right signals Sunday!

— John Ed

November 2, 1975

VIDEO-TAPE REPLAY

AUM has purchased a new video-tape machine. Dr. Don Chambless and Dr. Joe Elrod have been experimenting with some of its possibilities for use in the areas of athletics, such as tennis. They invited me out last week to experiment with the machine.

An instrument like a video-tape machine is very helpful in teaching somebody in an individual sport such as tennis. You can tell a person how to do it, but often the person doesn't have a grasp of his objective or his error until he sees it on film. A video-tape playback shows you exactly the way you are doing something. It leaves nothing to the imagination.

When he first started filming me, Dr. Elrod immediately noticed an obvious flaw in my footwork. He stopped for a minute and asked me if I was conscious of the fact that I was barely moving my left foot when hitting a forehand? I said no. Then he asked me, "Wouldn't you teach a student to hit a forehand by stepping forward with his left foot?" I said, "Of course."

It hit home with me because I know how you are supposed to teach someone to hit that tennis stroke, yet the film showed quite obviously that I wasn't doing it myself. In fact, I was not even aware that I was not doing it correctly. I guess this is the toughest part about being a minister. It is so easy to teach something, and then not follow that teaching yourself. And sometimes you do it without ever knowing it.

I am trying to examine my life to see the areas where my lifestyle is in contradiction to the teaching of the Word as I understand it. I'm finding that when I'm really honest, God has a way of "replaying" my strengths and weaknesses for me. And that's the first step toward change.

See you Sunday where you can see yourself at God's special place for "replays." And, oh, His work in this area is much beyond the experimental stage.

— John Ed

November 9, 1975

A PASSING FAD AND A LASTING FAITH

The hottest selling Christmas item in 1975 was the "mood ring." This ring is supposed to measure one's emotional state. A code card comes with the ring, indicating the meaning of the various colors of the ring. Each different color is supposed to detect such moods as happiness, sadness, anxiety, and passion.

But Dr. Glen Brown, Director of the Kent State Liquid Crystal Institute, says that the liquid crystals in the ring are highly sensitive to changes in temperature. The materials simply measure the blood flow through the finger as the pulse goes up — the color of the ring does too. Instead of measuring the mood, it only measures body temperature.

The "mood setters" for our Church for 1976 are listed on the back page of this bulletin. These are the people who are going to lead us to be what God wants us to be. By their personal examples and by their decisions for the program and ministry of this Church, I feel certain that Frazer's "mood" will communicate to Montgomery and the world the essentials of the Christian faith. The leaders will be installed at both morning worship services this Sunday.

The mood ring is a fad and it has been found to be faulty. Christianity is a lifestyle of faith — and it has been found to be foolproof!

— John Ed

January 11, 1976

MY LUCKY DAY

I just won over $200,000.00! I'm already making my retirement plans. Actually I haven't gotten the money yet, but I'm sure it will be here shortly because last week in my mailbox on Tuesday night I had three personal letters inviting me to send in a few coupons and claim my prize money. Mr. Robert Treller of Publisher's Clearing House is going to send me $100,000.00. Reader's Digest is going to send me $100.00 a month for the rest of my life, and McCalls is going to send me $35,000.00 in cash.

I really don't know what I'm going to do with all of this money. Each of the letters made it sound like there is no way that I could lose. It all looked like it was designed exactly for me. McCalls wrote, "Rev. Mathison, we would send off a check to 5208 Surrey Rd. for the full $35,000.00 — your's to use at once." One of the company's even showed a sample check made out to me with *my name* on it. Down at the bottom it was stamped non-negotiable.

These company's believe so much in the product they are selling that they're willing to give away these huge amounts of money to get people to try them. They really believe in their product! The McCalls offer sent two envelopes, one marked "yes" and one marked "no". When I started to put my sweepstake numbers in the envelope marked "no", meaning I did not want the free issue of McCalls, I opened the envelope and saw a little yellow piece of paper protruding which said, "Please don't say no, say maybe." They are so certain that if you get one issue you will want the rest of the issues to "keep on coming" — or forget to cancel them.

God believed so much in His way of life that He sent His Son to tell us about it. In Him He offers a personalized free gift of grace for everybody. It can't be bought, but everybody who receives it is a winner. And God's offer is not a "come-on" to sell you something else.

All of these offers carried with them a "promptness award". You can add to my money two sporty his 'n her's Chevettes plus a vacation with prize money because I responded before the deadline. I don't know what God's deadline is, but the time to respond to His Gift is now! Please, please, don't use the envelope marked no. I plead with you —say yes to Him.

If something unforeseeable happens and I don't win all that money, I'm still winning at the greatest Game I'm playing!

— John Ed
January 18, 1976

CHILD-LIKE FAITH

There's a little boy in our kindergarten who has an acute case of asthma. It has grown progressively worse during the past few months. To make matters more complicated the father has taken a job as a salesman which keeps him on the road several nights a week. This means that the mother has had the responsibility of staying up with a little six-year old at night when he is sick, then looking after a two-year old during the day. This can pretty well get the best of a mother in a short time.

Each day the kindergarten classes have a special time for prayer. When 15 kids gathered in a circle for prayer in Jason's room, the teacher asked if there were any requests. Jason asked the group to pray for his mother. The teacher responded by saying what's wrong with your mother (that's a dangerous question to ask a six year old because oftentimes they will tell you everything that's wrong in any home in the neighborhood)? Jason explained that he had been up most of the nights lately and his mother had had very little sleep. He asked the group to pray for him that he could get a good night's sleep and his mother could rest. A simple prayer you might say — but a class took it very seriously and asked God for this request.

That afternoon Jason went home and laid down on the couch about 4:30. He went to sleep. He slept through supper and all night long until 7:00 the next morning. The mother kept checking on him through the night because he had never slept like this! She was afraid something might be wrong with him. When she asked him how he felt the next morning, he said, "Fine". She said, "Do you realize that you slept all night?" He quickly replied, "Yes, I expected to." She said, "What do you mean?" He said, "Well, my class prayed for that". She said, "You mean your class prayed for you to get a good night's sleep?" Jason looked at his mother and said, "Yes Ma'am. We talked to Jesus about it and whenever you turn everything over to Jesus, He always takes care of it."

Most of us have some things we ought to turn over to Him. This would eliminate a lot of worries, ulcers, problems, and sleepless nights. I'm sure He can take care of anything.

And a child shall lead them . . .!

— *John Ed*

March 14, 1976

PRISONERS OF THE UNIMPORTANT

At the Montgomery Bicentennial Religious Heritage Rally on July 4th, I happened to be standing near Astronaut Frank Borman after the program when many people were coming up to get his autograph and take a picture. I was especially fascinated by one man who had a little boy about 5 years old. The father wanted his boy to meet Astronaut Borman and have a picture taken with him. But the father was having a hard time getting the attention of his little boy because he was more fascinated by a group of kids dressed like Indians and playing at the side of the stage. The father was desperately trying to tell his little boy about the important thing that Astronaut Borman has accomplished in going to the moon, but the little boy was more interested in the little kids playing.

This looked like a real parable of life to me. Here the little boy was in the presence of one of the most famous people in the world. Only a few people have ever been to the moon, and Astronaut Borman is one of that select group. And this little boy had the opportunity to meet him and have a picture taken with him. But the little boy was more interested in the childish games at the side of the stage than he was in meeting somebody great in life.

How many times are we like that little boy when God is trying to introduce us to some high and noble thought or some new revelation of his relationship to us? God is constantly trying to show us the people and places and things of life that so few experience. But instead we get ourselves bogged down in the mundane and meaningless issues of life. Our attention is so easily occupied by that which is commonplace rather than that which is extremely important. We become prisoners of the unimportant.

Any group of kids can dress up like Indians and play a make-believe game. It took a man like Borman to go to the moon, and while circling it on Christmas Eve deliver a great witness of a genuine faith. And we all had a chance to meet him.

Each day we have the opportunity to meet the One who hung the moon Borman circled, and is capable of releasing us from any prisons of the unimportant.

See you at the "meeting" and "releasing" place Sunday!

— *John Ed*

July 18, 1976

GIMMICKS, GROWTH, AND THE GOSPEL

During a recent seminar at Emory, several of us went out one night to see the Atlanta Braves play. I've often said that if I lived in Atlanta, I'm afraid that I would spend all my money watching the Braves, the Falcons, and the Hawks play ball.

I had heard a lot about the trouble that major league baseball is in financially. Salaries and expenses have escalated at a shocking pace while attendance has increased slowly — or none at all in some areas. Many sportsmen have said that the American pastime is in trouble.

I sensed part of the trouble at the Braves' game when I was constantly bombarded with all the gimmicks to get people to come to future games. For example, they advertised that at the next home game, eleven couples would be married at home plate before the ball game, and professional lady wrestlers would entertain after the ball - game. The next game would be frisbee night and everyone attending would receive a free frisbee. Then the next game would feature the president of the Atlanta Braves racing a sports editor of the *Atlanta Journal* on an ostrich, and was billed as the great ostrich race. Then the next night would be helmet night where all the kids sitting in a certain section would get a free batting helmet. And the next night would be bat night. Then the next night, senior citizens night, etc. I'd never seen so many gimmicks to get people to a game.

Now there's nothing wrong with gimmicks as long as people really have something worth experiencing once they attend. The gimmick is not the end, but the means to something else. I'm not opposed to the church using incentives like perfect attendance pins and attendance promotions to get people to church. However, the church must have something vital to offer the people once they come. The growth of an institution does not rest in gimmicks, but in the experience of the participation.

I would suggest that major league baseball look beyond its' gimmicks to its' main offering to the American public. And the church needs to do the same.

See you at the place Sunday that's short on gimmicks, but long on Good News!

— John Ed

August 8, 1976

WHERE GOLD MEDAL TRAINING STARTS

Bela Karolyi scouts kindergartens for gymnasts. He looks for boys and girls who have special skills at this age and then tries to develop them.

One day he saw a kindergarten girl playing at gymnastics at recess. He recognized her skill but when the bell rang he lost sight of the child. He started looking from room to room but did not find her. On the third trip to the classrooms he asked who loves gymnastics, "Oui, Oui", shouted a young girl and her friend. The young girl was Nadia Comaneci. Bela started working with Nadia because he recognized her innate ability at her young age.

In Montreal this summer Nadia Comaneci received the first perfect score of 10 ever awarded in the Olympics. She went on to receive 7 perfect 10's in gymnastics. Four of these perfect 10's were on the uneven bars and three of the 10's were on the four inch wide beam — an incredible performance.

Bela Karolyi contends that if you can take a child at the tender kindergarten age, the best skills of their life can be developed. Each child living in the homes of the people of Frazer has untapped resources of creativity and potential. There is an "imprisoned splendor" in each person. I hope all parents will carefully observe and bring their children into the kind of Christian training at an early age that can help develop this great potential. God has a lot of Gold Medals for life if we are perceptive and persistant enough to get boys and girls into the proper training at an early age.

This Sunday is promotion Sunday in our Sunday School. It is an excellent time to look around your neighborhood (or home) and enroll some children (or youth and adults) in a program of Christian education. No one is to young or too old for Sunday School!

See you at the place Sunday that provides training for Gold Medals!

— John Ed

August 29, 1976

CHURCH OR MUSEUM

I was in Pensacola, Florida recently and visited Seville Square, which is right on the edge of downtown Pensacola. It is an old historic area that has deteriorated, yet recent interest has been shown in perserving some of the historical spots and restoring some of the old buildings. What has happened is almost unbelievable. There are a lot of little low rent shotgun houses in that area which could have been bought four or five years ago for about four or five thousand dollars. Now, with the interest in that area, these houses are being sold for forty-five to fifty thousand dollars. New businesses are taking these old buildings and renovating them and making offices out of them.

Right off Seville Square I noticed a historic old church. Someone said that it was the first Episcopal Church in the United States. Services were authorized to be held on that spot in 1763 and by 1779 a small congregation had been organized. In 1827, a pastor was appointed and the building was constructed in 1832 (these dates are from memory). I immediately went to the church because I was interested in it. Then I discovered a sign over the door indicating that it was no longer a church, but now was a historic museum. The thing that really floored me was the hours of operation on the front door of the church. It said, "Closed on Sundays and Mondays."

Here is a great historic church — but it is no longer a church. Somewhere in it's history it failed to have a ministry to the people around it, so eventually it's ministry became obsolete. Now it's just a historic museum that attracts people who are interested in the things of the past.

When a church ceases to minister to people, it becomes a museum. Our church has a tremendous responsibility to this section of Montgomery. May we stand strong and tall in accepting and dispensing our responsibility to be God's instrument at this location.

See you at the place Sunday that's "Open" 24 hours a day!

— John Ed

September 5, 1976

SEVEN STEPS TO A SUPER SEVENTY-SEVEN

I. RECOMMIT YOUR LIFE TO CHRIST EACH DAY
   (Matthew 16:24)

II. ATTEND WORSHIP AND SUNDAY SCHOOL EACH SUNDAY
   (Acts 2:42)

III. READ AND STUDY THE BIBLE DAILY—AND APPLY IT
   (II Timothy 3:15)

IV. PRAY EACH DAY
   (I Timothy 2:8)

V. WRITE 1ST CHECK EACH WEEK (OR MONTH)
   REPRESENTING 10% OF INCOME AS TITHE
   (Malachi 3:10)

VI. APPLY CHRIST'S STANDARD TO HUMAN
   RELATIONSHIPS—BOTH PERSONAL AND SOCIAL
   (I John 4:20)

VII. SHARE YOUR FAITH BY LIP AND BY LIFE
   (Acts 5:42)

God wants 77 to be the best year ever for you and me! I've tried to put together these seven steps to make it that for us. Place these suggested steps on your refrigerator or bulletin board. Place a check (literally or mentally) at the end of the week if you've taken each step.

Each step is important — none should be omitted.

See you at the place Sunday that is *stepping* forward for a Super 77

— John Ed

January 2, 1977

CONDUCT

My seven-year-old son, Si, who is a first grader, brought his report card home last week. He had good grades. First graders also receive a conduct grade for each subject. In looking at the conduct grades, Si made all B's.

I know P.K.'s (preacher's kids) have a reputation of being "mischievous". Since I'm a P.K., I feel we learn most of this from associating with all the church member's kids! I also remembered some words from Si's kindergarten teacher last year when she very tactfully said, "Rev. Mathison, Si is an intelligent child with high capabilities, but if he is not properly challenged he could be a discipline problem." I got her message. Then she added, "But I'm sure he will never be the problem that you were!"

So I sat down to talk with Si about his conduct grades. I showed him all the A's and B's he had made in the other subjects and asked him what had happened in conduct. He thought for a minute, then with an astonished look on his face, innocently exclaimed, "Golly, daddy, I don't ever remember going to conduct!"

Si didn't realize that conduct wasn't a class that you go to, but covered his entire activity at school. A lot of people think that Christianity is conduct exhibited when you go to "religious" functions. But the real test of Christianity is our conduct in all aspects of life. Christianity is not something you go to — but it is who you are.

Sidewalk sermons speak more loudly and with greater clarity than do pulpit sermons. Christianity is not an area of life alongside work, leisure, hobby, family, etc. It is a part of all life.

See you at the place Sunday that's emphasizing a better grade of conduct!

— *John Ed*

February 6, 1977

33

WHOSE VOICE IS THAT?

Betsy Crawford is the five-year-old daughter of John and Catherine Crawford. She is a faithful attender at worship but sometimes has a difficult time seeing over the big adults sitting in front of her. When Jack Thompson first came here he sat with me behind the pulpit and used the pulpit mike. For the past few months he has been sitting with Joe Pat behind the lectern (I'm sure my singing had nothing to do with his move).

The first Sunday that Jack started to pray using the lectern mike his voice came booming through the public address system. Betsy looked over the shoulders of the fellow in front of her and saw no one standing at the pulpit. She quickly said to her daddy, "Who is that?" John quietly responded, "That's Rev. Thompson." A look of relief crossed Betsy's face as she said, "Whew, I thought it was God."

Most of us have never heard God speak in an audible voice. But I'm convinced that I've heard Him speak through the voices of many people. I do not experience God as some Cosmic Being out in the universe, but rather as One who is working through people and events to speak to me in my own situation.

When God wanted to say something to us about Himself, He wrapped up His message in the form of a person — Jesus Christ. I believe that one way God wants to deliver His message today is through people (both by lip and lifestyle). I feel that God wants to speak even more to today's world through His people.

Betsy, I know what you and your daddy meant by your response, but I think you were more correct than he. I think it was God speaking through one of His servants. God will be speaking through him Sunday morning at both morning worship services. I'll be preaching at my Dad's church in Panama City.

Be listening . . . . and speaking — God has a lot to say!

— John Ed

February 13, 1977

34

BARKING UP THE SAME TREE

While making a routine visit to Jackson Hospital recently, I decided to park my car on Pine Street beside Oak Park. As I walked up to the red light at the intersection of Forest Avenue and Pine Street, I saw an elderly lady looking around, obviously lost. I stopped to ask if I could help her and she said that she was a visitor in town and somebody had told her there was a drugstore there where she could get some "get well" cards.

I explained that there was a drugstore adjacent to Jackson Hospital and pointed towards it and asked her if she could see a red service truck. When she indicated that she could not see the truck (which was only a few feet away) I knew that her eyesight was very poor. I offered to help her across Forest Avenue. As we started walking down Pine Street toward the drugstore I wondered how she would find her way home. When I questioned her about this she indicated that it would be no trouble because she said, "The Lord is my Shepherd and He leadeth me."

Well, I appreciated her faith but I felt like the Lord had put me there at that moment to help her get to the drugstore, so I escorted her to it. She began to tell me about all the good things the Lord was doing for her in her life. I was impressed by her sincerity and deep faith. An elderly lady who could hardly see or walk, yet her conversation centered on the many things for which she had to be grateful.

She then asked who I was and what I did. When I told her I was a Methodist preacher a big smile broke across her face and she said, "Sonny (I'm sorry I told you her eyesight was poor), we're barking up the same tree."

I was glad to be "barking up the same tree" with a lady with that kind of attitude and faith. She had the kind of spirit I want as I move on in years.

I also learned that that lady needed me to help her. I would interpret her understanding that the Lord was leading her to mean that the Lord led me to that street corner and used me to lead her. In fact, I'm seeing more and more where God's leadership and work is being done through His people.

See you at the place Sunday where we're all barking up the same tree!

— *John Ed*

March 13, 1977

ACCESSIBILITY

President Carter, in a deliberate and intentional effort to "stay close to the people" collaborated with CBS to initiate a program whereby Americans could call in on the telephone and ask him any question or tell him anything they had on their mind. Last week 42 Americans were able to talk to the President on the telephone. But there were also 9,499,958 disappointed people who got a busy signal when they called.

It would be a great thrill to talk to the President of the United States. But I am reminded that one of our emphases and disciplines during Lent is prayer. Through this we have the opportunity to talk with Someone far more important than the President each day. He is very much interested in answering our questions and hearing what we have on our minds. Nobody gets a busy signal with Him!

President Carter had several of his aides standing nearby to help him with questions that he could not answer. Several times he had to refer the questions to them. God has the answers to all the pressing questions that we have. Sometimes God's answer isn't exactly the answer that we want to hear, but He has an answer. He doesn't have to consult with anybody about the right answer.

A lot of people who called the President received a wrong number. There was some fellow in Indiana whose telephone rang all day long. He had the same number as the President, except for the area code. People were really disappointed when they heard his voice rather than the President's. In prayer we don't have to worry about disappointments. Neither do we have to worry about wrong numbers.

I appreciate the President's effort to make himself accessible to the American people. I'm even more grateful for a God who is making Himself accessible for all people. His accessibility is not limited to television scheduling, but is available at any time. And His accessibility is not by telephone, but is in person.

See you at the place Sunday where the Frazer family expresses appreciation for His accessibility!

— *John Ed*

March 20, 1977

36

HEADACHES AND HEARTACHES

Recently I went into a hospital room and visited a lady who was suffering with intense pain, probably from migraine headaches. The doctor had her hooked up to an interesting little instrument to help relieve the pain.

The instrument is a Transcutaneous Nerve Stimulator, which transmits an electrical signal through the skin to the appropriate underlying nerves to prevent the message of pain from reaching the brain. It intercepts the pain before it reaches the brain. Actually this basic technique was first reported by Roman and Greek physicians about 254 A.D. while using tubs of water filled with electric fish to relieve the pain of gout, headache, and other etiologies. I understand that medical authorities have been using TNS for about ten years as a nondrug diagnositc tool and for the relief of chronic pain. Reports have shown TNS to be a safe, benign, effective method of pain control with no known side effects.

This particular instrument is manufactured by Staodyn, which literally means "to stop pain and distress." It is a very small instrument and can be attached with a leather belt clip. It is restricted to sale and use by or on the order of a physician.

Intercepting pain before it makes its' impression on the brain is a great step forward. I wish something could be invented to intercept pain signals before they reach the heart. Every week I confront so many people who suffer not from headaches, but heartaches. They experience disappointment, discouragement, doubt, disillusionment, and some face death. I find that heartaches are much more severe than headaches.

On this Passion Sunday, I am reminded that Jesus said, "Let not your hearts be troubled..." In another place he said, "sorrow has filled your hearts ... but I will send the Comforter to you ..." Jesus doesn't relieve us of the heartaches of life, but he does give us the strength and courage to bear them. God's love in our hearts doesn't intercept the pain, but it does dull it and help us deal with it.

See you at the place Sunday where we are trained to both prevent and handle inevitable heartaches!

— *John Ed*

March 27, 1977

"I DON'T LIKE DEATH"

Mr. Ed Emfinger built a nice little birdhouse and placed it in the backyard for my family. We've enjoyed the birds who make their home there. Last week my seven-year-old son came in with a little bird egg that he found on the ground. It was cracked. Inside was a little half-formed baby bird. As Joan held it in the palm of her hand, my children started asking questions about why things have to die. In a few minutes, Si took the little bird in his hand and sincerely said, "Gee, I really wish we could bring you back to life." Then he looked at me as if I could do something, but I was speechless and helpless.

About an hour later that afternoon we found two dead baby kittens. The pregnant mother cat had taken up at our house earlier and we knew that she had had her kittens but could not find them. The death of these three animals came too close together. Si was both mad and sad, but he expressed our feelings when he said, "Daddy, I just don't like death."

This Easter Day we celebrate the life of a Man who didn't like death either. And He had a Father who could do something about death. On Friday of Holy Week men decided to do away with God by killing His Son, but on Easter God claimed His greatest victory when death was defeated as He raised Jesus from the dead. God showed the world that He's not interested in funerals, but resurrection.

I'm looking forward to celebrating God's victory over death with you. I hope you will be conscious of our changed schedule for Easter morning. Our first worship service will begin at 8:15, 30 minutes earlier than usual. There will also be a worship service at 9:30. Sunday School will begin 15 minutes earlier at 9:30 and proceed until 10:30 as usual. Also let me remind you that there is parking available on the ball field if the parking lot is full.

I'm glad God didn't like death. I wish I could have helped my children bring that little bird back to life, but only Jesus had a Father who could do that. And when He gives Life to us, it is forever ... and ever ... and ever.

See you at the resurrection place Sunday!

— *John Ed*

April 10, 1977

38

WHAT TIME IS IT?

A man was late to a meeting last week. He checked his time on the Alabama National Bank clock next to TG&Y. What he didn't realize was that the power had been off in East Montgomery for 46 minutes, and he was relying on that clock as a guide for his schedule. He leisurely strolled into the meeting just before the benediction!

Jesus said, "You are the light of the world." Our lives as Christians, like that clock, are in places of high visibility to provide light, give direction, and serve as a guide for people designing their lifestyles. And if our lives, like that clock, are not accurate then we will throw a lot of people late in life.

One of the big problems of the clock was that it was almost accurate. If it had been six hours off, nobody would have paid any attention to it. But it was just a few minutes off. If we "almost" let our lights shine, we are most misleading.

The clock also flashes the temperature with the time. Once the power came back on it did not affect the accurate reporting of the temperature. This would also lead one to think that the time should also be accurate. Some people feel like the church has done it's job if it simply measures the moral climate of society. Our task as Christians is not only to measure the moral and spiritual temperature of society but also to serve as a guide to get people where they ought to be at the proper time and place.

Last Sunday was another record breaking day as we had 37 people join the church! Under Jack Thompson's leadership, evangelism is appealing, effective and accurately communicated.

See you at the place Sunday where the Power is on for reporting the right temperature and time!

— *John Ed*

April 24, 1977

ONLY ONE WAY TO GO — UP

Week before last America woke up to the TV coverage of George Willig's daring attempt to climb the 110 story World Trade Center in New York City. At 6:40 a.m. he had already started up the side of the building before security guards and police noticed him. Immediately they shouted for him to climb down. He looked at the confused authorities below and shouted to them, "There is only one way to go, and that is up."

Last week ended the 149th session of the Alabama-West Florida Annual Conference. This week marks the beginning of New Conference Year. Frazer had a remarkable report for the Annual Conference, but I hope our spirit is not simply one of satisfaction with last year's report, but one of dedication and commitment to improve for this year. I know our spirit will be, "There is only one way to go, and that is up."

I want to see us move forward in our individual commitment to Jesus Christ and His church — set higher goals for our personal evangelism — become more sensitive to social issues confronting us — become more involved in community ministries — give more to World Hunger — increase our Sunday School and worship attendance — go beyond the minimal financial commitment of 10% — win more unchurched people on Profession of Faith — grow in every aspect of Christian responsibility.

As individuals and as a Church we face the danger of resting on the record of the past and settling down in the current stage of our Christian growth. If we do this, we become stagnant, stale and ultimately ineffective.

Jesus always calls people to move forward in the faith. In the Book of Acts there is the record of how the early church was always moving in one direction — forward. Christians and churches always grow — or die.

See you at the place Sunday that is going only one way — up!

— John Ed

June 12, 1977

WHO SPEAKS WITH AUTHORITY?

On Wednesday, July 13th at 3:00 p.m., Mr. Charles Frank Luce, Chairman of the Board of Consolidated Edison Company, made the following statement to the people of New York. "The Con Ed System is in the best shape in 15 years and there's no problem for the summer". Five hours later, 9 million people were left in the dark as the New York area was suddenly deprived of electrical power, probably because of lightening.

The whole city shut down. Mayor Abe Beame declared a state of emergency. He criticized the power system by saying, "We can't tolerate in this age of technology, a power system that can shut down the nation's largest city".

Five hours earlier, New York City had been assured of no potential problems by a man in the best position to make such a statement. Mr. Luce had at his fingertips all the advanced technological data on which to make his statement, and this city had every human reason to believe him.

Even in an age of advanced technology, we are not as smart as we think. What happened in New York should cause us to look at other aspects of life. We spend billions of dollars in the defense of our nation, but is this where a nation puts its ultimate confidence for defense? Our nation's economy operates to the rhythm of the stock exchange, but is this where ultimate security is found? We marvel at medical advancement, but can medicine bring a person to wholeness in itself? We almost worship our scientific discoveries and skills, but is this where the ultimate meaning of life is found? We enjoy the most highly developed communication system known to man, yet we have trouble talking to each other.

New York City should remind us that no expert has the final word on any subject. God created all things. Ultimate truth and meaning are in His hands. I'm appreciative of technological advancement, but it must be seen against the backdrop of God's providence. God has the last word!

God speaks with all authority when He offers all cities and people a Power System that is never interrupted. And blackouts are not even in God's vocabulary.

See you at the place Sunday where people are listening to One who can really speak with authority!

— John Ed
July 24, 1977

41

ORIGINALS AND CARBONS

I was in an office recently of one of our church members. While waiting for him to make a phone call I became interested in the typing of his secretary. I noticed she made some errors while typing a letter but when I looked at the finished copy I could not see where the errors had been made.

I asked her about this and she demonstrated her new self-correcting typewriter. Whenever she made a mistake she simply pressed a key and typed over the mistake exactly as it had been made, and it removed the mistake from the paper. She could then type in the correct letter. You could not detect the error on the finished copy of the letter. I was fascinated by this because all typewriters I've used made a lot of mistakes!

I then saw the carbon copy of the letter she kept for her own file and the errors were very evident on the carbon copy. She quickly explained to me that the typewriter can correct the original copy so that you don't notice it, but it does not correct the carbon copy.

God erases the mistakes, errors, and sins of our life when we confess them. He goes over them exactly and removes them and forgives us for them. But our confession and forgiveness does not remove the imprint those errors make on our children and friends and those who are looking to us for leadership. The errors are corrected in our lives, but we never know how many carbon copies have been patterned after us.

Stop — think before you do something questionable. It may not show up on your original, but you never know how many carbons you are making.

See you Sunday at the place where the originals for better carbons are being made!

— John Ed

September 18, 1977

WHAT A RECORD!

Mrs. Bonnie Marvin and her two daughters, Iola and Anna, have attended every baseball game that the Dodgers have played in Los Angeles since moving there from Brooklyn in 1958. Over 1600 games and they have never missed a one. That's an incredible record, especially when you consider the fact that Mrs. Marvin is 93 years old and her daughters are 69 and 65! They are always in their seats on the first row of aisle 41, midway between third base and the left field foul line.

Mrs. Marvin, because of her 93 years of age, says that sometimes she doesn't feel well and the walk from the parking lot up the steps to the stadium is hard on her. To avoid the crowd, she arrives 1 1/2 hours early. She even said that she sometimes had headaches so bad she could hardly hold her head up, but she wouldn't dream of missing a game. The Marvins only get sick when the Dodgers are playing on the road!

That record of commitment to a baseball team ought to make every Christian stop and think. We are commited to Someone far more important than a baseball team, yet how many Christians do you know have that kind of record for attending church? Very few Christians are "where the action is," regardless of weather, headaches, etc.

Now the Marvins aren't fair weather fans. The Dodgers haven't always been winners since moving West from Brooklyn in 1958. But the Marvins have been right there for every game. Even last year when 69 year-old Iola was hit in the face by a foul ball and needed five stitches, she was back in her seat the next day!

93 years old — but I bet I know where she'll be when the National Anthem is sung for each World Series Game at Dodger Stadium. I wonder where most Christians will be when the Call to Worship is sung this Sunday.

See you in your place Sunday regardless of weather, headaches, etc. (all over 93 years old excused) . . .!

— John Ed

October 16, 1977

FROM SPECTATOR TO PARTICIPANT

Last weekend was Si's eighth birthday, so I told him that I would do anything with him that he wanted to do. He quickly said that he wanted to go ice skating. I had oftentimes stood around the rink at the new Mall and watched people ice skate but I never had the courage to try it myself. Now I had no choice.

I quickly discovered that ice skating is alot more fun than just watching. It took some courage to take that first step and get on the ice, but once I did it was loads of fun. I really don't know anything about ice skating. I never even figured out how to keep score — but I think if par was 72 (falls), I might have been just under par! Several church members enjoyed seeing me get up from that "cool" position.

There were some people skating who spent all of their time near the edge of the rink holding the rail. They were afraid to venture out on to the ice. They had the rank of spectators, but still just walked on the ice holding to the rail. Then I discovered there were some people skating who were quite good at it. They were obviously enjoying it more than anyone else.

I SHARE is God's opportunity to get us out of the rank of spectators, off the rails where it is safe, and onto the rink of sacrificial service where the real joy is.

There was one man in particular who was quite good and was practicing some very difficult turns and techniques. He actually fell a few times and some of the kids laughed at him, but he kept trying until he got it right. I could see and sense the satisfaction on his face. I SHARE in God's opportunity to challenge us to risk new areas of commitment and sharing. We might fall some, but God reserves the greatest joy and satisfaction for those who risk the most and trust Him for success.

I also have to remember that it was my young son who talked me into going ice skating. I have learned that God often uses boys and girls and youth to lead parents and adults to a more satisfying relationship with Christ and His church. They are taking some big risks — and getting big results.

See you at the "risking place" Sunday that's reducing the ranks of spectators and rail walkers!

— John Ed

October 30, 1977

BUILDING UP OR BREAKING DOWN

Last week they moved a big 40 ton crane onto the church property. It has an 80 ft. boom on it stretching up to the sky. It will be used to put the second story beams in place for the new building.

I don't know where the crane was used before it was brought to Frazer, but when it arrived it had those large steel balls that are used for tearing down buildings. When I inquired about them I was told that they were called "headache balls" (I didn't have to ask how they got that name). Each of those big steel balls weighed several hundred pounds.

I was curious about the crane because it will be very helpful in setting the beams to put the roof on our new building. But if the wrong person got behind the controls of that crane, it would be used to tear down not only the new building, but also the existing sanctuary and educational space. In fact I asked the foreman how long it would take somebody to tear down all of our buildings using that crane. He looked at me and smiled and said, "It could be done in a couple of days".

Beautiful buildings that have taken months and months and months to build, yet they can be torn down in a couple of days. That just doesn't seem right. The real Church (not brick and mortar) also takes a long time to build. But that Church can also be torn apart very quickly.

Each of us is like that crane — we have a capacity to build or tear down. Building requires commitment, prayer, and a lot of hard work. Little skill is required for tearing down — all it takes is a jealous heart, an unforgiving spirit, a critical attitude, a tendency to have hurt feelings, "I'm more spiritual than you" communication, a tendency to repeat something that might not be completely true, etc.

Be a part of the building team this year. Replace any "headache balls" with constructive attachments for witness and work.

See you at the *building* place Sunday!

— John Ed

January 15, 1978

45

THE ENERGY CRISIS

The current coal worker's strike has led to an energy crisis in America. Stockpiles are at the critical stage and the first phase emergency measures are being introduced this week.

This energy crisis in the church is equally as critical. Visits not made, clothing not provided, food not offered, witness not made, justice not practiced — people are using their energy for other things.

I would like to propose this 7 point plan for Frazer to help combat the energy crisis.

(1) Increase outdoor advertising. Witnessing "outdoors" in the world is more important than "indoors" at church.

(2) Voluntarily "cut forward" your time of service to those in need by 20%.

(3) Leave your lights on all the time. Remember, you are the light of the world.

(4) Raise the thermostat of your "warm heart experience."

(5) Use mass worship systems weekly — not just private worship.

(6) Don't use car pools coming to church. Fill your car with unchurched people.

(7) Fix the drapes of your home so the Son can shine in.

The energy crisis must be alleviated, and I don't think God has a Taft-Hartly Act to do that. He has you and me — we are His plan!

— *John Ed*

March 12, 1978

EMBARRASSING MOMENT

Last week President Carter entertained Romanian President Nico-lae Ceausesce in Washington. At a State dinner in honor of the visiting President, the band played what they thought was the Romanian National Anthem. When President Ceausesce and his party members looked confused, it was discovered that the song the band was playing was discontinued as the National Anthem 30 years ago. It was an embarrassing moment for everyone concerned. Someone failed to do their "homework." A mistake like that probably increased the unemployment in Washington.

Sometimes Christian witness is an embarrassment because we Christians fail to do our "homework." Our lack of preparation creates confusion and negative results.

The church today needs to be speaking the language that people understand. The church needs to be developing strategies of ministry that are relevant in 1978. We need to be constantly studying better and more effective ways to communicate the "good news."

Some "homework" that each of us need to do in our personal Christian witness is daily Bible study. We have to know the Book before we can share it with others. We need to spend more time in prayer. We need to be more perceptive to places where God's spirit might use us.

Our lifestyles in Christian living must enhance rather than hinder our Christian witness. Last week there were representatives from Trinidad in Montgomery to study the Alabama Ethics Commission. As Christians our "ethics" are being studied and observed everyday by people around us. The best witness is one where people see it demonstrated in a lifestyle.

Witness is our most important responsibility and opportunity. Be prepared to do it effectively.

See you at the "preparing" place Sunday!

— *John Ed*

April 23, 1978

SPREAD THE WORD

When is peanut butter not peanut butter? The Federal Government answered that question recently when the Food and Drug Administration said peanut butter had to be at least 90% peanuts and must meet certain nutritional requirements. Products which don't meet that standard will have to have new names.

At this time, on a voluntary basis, manufacturers can sell peanut products similar to peanut butter with any amount of peanuts, but they will have to be called "peanut spread" and the label will have to list the percentage of peanuts included. If they fail to meet the nutritional requirements for peanut butter, the name will have to be "imitation peanut butter."

Now when kids (and parents) eat America's favorite sandwich, they can be assured of getting the real thing. All imitations must be designated as such.

It's tragic that there is a lot of living today that goes under the label of Christianity, but does not meet the minimum requirements and is really an imitation. There are too many people who "talk" but don't "walk" the faith. Too many people limit their Christianity to Sunday. This can be very confusing to new Christians and to outsiders because no one is wearing a label of "imitation Christian" or "Christian spread".

While peanut butter can get along with 90% peanuts, Christianity requires 100% commitment. Jesus said that a man must love God with *all* his heart, *all* his mind, *all* his soul, and *all* his strength (Mark 12:30). Jesus talked about the rewards of full commitment when Peter said that they had forsaken *all* and followed Him (Matt. 19:27) Jesus invites us to "Come after Me" — no place for spread or imitation.

I feel that it is far more important for people to get the real thing when they are looking for Christianity than when they are eating peanut butter. The only kind of spread we need is the kind that gets the Word to more people!

See you at the place Sunday that is "spreading the Word"!

— *John Ed*

July 9, 1978

THE WHOLE TRUTH

I was recently a part of a group discussing the US Open Tennis Tournament won by Jimmy Conners. In an early match he was almost upset as he was extended to 3 sets by Pat Dupre of Anniston, Alabama. When someone asked me what I thought about Dupre's play, I casually commented that I had beaten him the last time we played. There were stunned looks — followed by silence.

Now what I said was the truth. There was nothing false about it. I did beat Dupre the last time we played — but it was not the whole truth in the context of the conversation. I did not say (at least immediately) that is was several years ago that I beat him in a practice set when he was just a kid beginning tennis. My statement was true, but did not reflect the whole truth.

It is very dangerous to teach or repeat things that might not represent the whole truth. Beware of half-truths — you might have the wrong half! Be sure something is completely true before you repeat it. In some beauty salons the talk alone is enough to curl your hair! The telephone can be a more deadly instrument for destroying people than firearms. In some houses the telephone picks up more dirt than the vacuum cleaner.

The Bible is God's source book of truth, yet parts of it can be taken out of context. I have heard recently some foolish lines of thought which take parts of verses out of context and are interpreted in a manner inconsistent with the whole Biblical revelation. Just because the Bible indicates that Solomon served in David's court doesn't mean that they were playing tennis! Partial verses or sentences taken out of context can be used to prove almost the opposite point.

Be sure to get the whole truth in all you do. Our command as Christians is to "go," not gossip.

See you at the place Sunday that is striving to learn and project the "whole truth"!

— John Ed

September 24, 1978

NAMES AND NUMBERS

Did you read about Eugene Jerome Perdue, a resident of Florida, who last month became the father of his sixth child? He named the boy Eugene Jerome Perdue. There is not much unusual about that except that he had already named his other five children Eugene Jerome Perdue also — and three of them are girls! So the new baby becomes Eugene Jerome Perdue VII.

When asked why he named each of the children after himself he replied, "I love Me". It must be awfully confusing when someone calls the Perdue residence and asks for Eugene. Mr. Perdue said that he had no trouble identifying his children because he just refers to them by numbers. A typical conversation must sound something like this, "Five, tell six to leave three alone, and tell two to give seven a bottle." I wonder what he calls his wife??

In sharp contrast to this the Christmas narrative tells us that a child was born and they named Him Jesus because He would "save His people from their sins." The name Jesus was carefully selected because it pointed to the ministry and mission of the One who was born on Christmas Day.

God's naming of His Son was not a selfish matter, but even His name indicated that God was giving Him to the world. And that name insures that none of us ever becomes a number, because it teaches us that God knows each of us by name and not by number. Regardless of how large the world grows, God is still interested in us as individuals.

The Christmas spirit is wrapped up in Him who was born in a manger — He did not come to the world for His own benefit but, "that whosoever believes in Him should not perish, but have everlasting life." What will your Christmas and my Christmas be like? Is it a self-centered celebration — or does our spirit bear witness to His Spirit who was born? A few ways we can express that spirit is through our gifts to the Methodist Children's Home in Selma, through helping some family less fortunate than we, and through giving the best of our talents and treasures through the church for God's witness.

See you at the place Sunday where you have a *name* and not a *number* because God loved you more than He loved Himself!

— John Ed

December 17, 1978

TWO BOYS WORKING TOGETHER

During Christmas one of the programs of the rehabilitation work in Montgomery was the emphasis on recycling usable goods to make decorations. Handicapped people were encouraged to take litter and make it into glitter.

A group of children were encouraged to display their creativity and the best Christmas decoration would be rewarded with a silver dollar. One boy in a wheelchair who had no arms and legs was excited about some ideas that he had for making decorations. His mind was churning with creative ideas. Suddenly a little fellow walked over and stood right in front of his face to read his lips because he was deaf and couldn't hear. When he "heard" his friend, he became excited and said, "He has the ideas in his mind and the ears to hear, and I have the hands and feet to carry out his ideas so we'll work together and win the prize."

And work together they did — they not only won the silver dollar for their particular group, but they also won the best window decoration for the downtown stores and received a Certificate of Appreciation from the Chamber of Commerce. With each having his own handicap, neither could have made the decorations. But working together, they formed an unbeatable team!

Each of us has handicaps and limitations. No one person can carry out the ministry of the church. But my understanding of Church is that we are people who work together and allow our mutual strengths and weaknesses to mesh. We "bear one anothers burdens...". By ourselves we can do very little, but together God can work miracles through us!

If you will provide the thinking and the ears, I'll provide the hands and the feet — and there is just no limit to what God can do through us! He can recycle unused talent and make a lot of litter glitter for Him.

See you at the "together" place Sunday!

— *John Ed*

February 18, 1979

DON'T FOOL AROUND WITH LIFE AND DEATH

Two lawyers, John Carroll and Al Pennington, have filed a motion asking for a stay of execution in the case of John Lewis Evans, III, convicted murderer. The strange part of the case is that John Lewis Evans, III, does not want a stay of execution and wants to die.

Carroll and Pennington contend they have found an error that deprived Evans of his substantial constitutional rights. The error was not discovered until after the execution date of April 6th was set by the Alabama Supreme Court.

Carroll and Pennington have been questioned repeatedly as to why they have given so much time and effort to try to save the life of a man who doesn't care whether or not his life is saved. Their answers have been based on humanitarian efforts and their responsibilities as attorneys.

Lent reminds us how a Man went to every extent to provide new life for people who did not deserve new life. He went beyond finding technicalities in the law or humanitarian interests — He went to the point that He was willing to die so that people who deserve to die might live. No person deserves to live because of the sin in his life, yet this Man died so that if convicted sinful man would "change his mind," he could have life both here on earth and life eternal.

I don't know what will happen April 6th — whether or not John Lewis Evans, III, will die or not. I do know what can happen in your life and mine — our execution can be permanently stayed by the grace given to us in Jesus Christ!

Sunday is April Fool's Day — watch out for all the tricks! Harmless tricks are fun, but don't be "fooled" into thinking there is any other way to life except through the pardon offered by Jesus Christ. I guess we have April Fool's Day so we don't discriminate against those who ignore Good Friday and Easter.

See you at the place Sunday where we worship a Man who went beyond the law to save us, not only for this life, but for all of life — no fooling!!

— *John Ed*

April 1, 1979

FORMING FRIENDSHIP

Bob Hayes, one of the greatest athletes in the 1960's, found himself on an April day in 1979 confessing to and being convicted for selling narcotics to an undercover agent. He received two five-year prison sentences.

He was considered the world's fastest human. He ran the 100-yard dash in 9.1 and the 100 meters in 10 seconds flat. In the 1964 Olympics in Tokyo, he won a gold medal in the 100 meter and anchored the 400 meter relay team. He was clocked at an incredible 8.5 seconds in the final 110 yards! He became an outstanding wide receiver for the Dallas Cowboys. He was one of the best known and most quoted athletes. His college coach, Jake Gaither, said that if there had ever been a kid he wanted to adopt, it was Bob Hayes.

Bob Hayes went from the pinnacle of glory to a prison where last month they took his fingerprints and sprayed him for lice. What happened? Nobody knows for sure, but Dallas Cowboy President, Tex Schramm, testified that Hayes did not have the ability to select good friends. The people with whom he associated led him into trouble and gave him bad advice in his business dealings. Last Spring he formed a friendship with a man who led him into the drug traffic.

Our friends and associations are so important. We generally reflect the attitudes and lifestyles of those with whom we spend time. I talk with so many young people who "got mixed up with the wrong crowd," then their actions became mixed up. I have talked with so many couples whose marriages are broken up or on the rocks because they "went along with their friends and did what they did." There are so few places in Montgomery where single young adults can go to meet the kind of people who make good friends.

It is important for all of us to make friends through church channels. We need to be involved with people who are going the way God wants us to go. A Sunday School Class is so important. We need to take an objective look at the people with whom we associate because there is a good chance that's what we will be like in the future.

I had always admired Bob Hayes. I wish he had known a special friend of mine, and through Him developed his friendships! It would have made all the difference in the world!

See you at the place Sunday where "good friendships" are formed!

— *John Ed*

May 6, 1979

LITTLE THINGS MEAN A LOT

Melchor Javair and his wife were living in Manilla, Philippines and were expecting a $1,000 draft from a relative in Pittsburgh. As the clerk at the Mellon Bank of Pittsburgh typed the foreign draft, she made a small error by accidently typing 3 extra zeros. Now zeros stand for nothing, but if those zeros are put in the wrong place they can make a big difference. That small mistake turned a $1,000 draft into a $1,000,000 draft!

You can image something of the surprise of Javair and his wife when they received the draft! When the Mellon Bank caught up with them 12 days later they said they had spent most of the funds. They offered to return a small fraction, provided the bank would not sue them, however, the bank proceeded with a lawsuit which is now tangled in legal spaghetti.

Little things might seem insignificant, but if they occur at the wrong time they bring large results. A base hit may do no harm, unless the bases are loaded. Running a caution light may be of no consequence, unless someone else is running the same caution light at the same time. An unexpected loss of temper may appear harmless, unless a young family member happens to be observing. Constructive criticism about another person may seem right unless the wrong person hears it and embellishes the story.

Little things have such potential power. James reminds us that a tiny rudder can make a huge ship turn wherever the pilot wants it to go. You can make a large horse turn around and go wherever you want by means of a small bit in his mouth. And even though the tongue is a small thing, it can do enormous damage. He compares the tongue to a spark setting off a forest fire and says that it can turn our whole life into a blazing flame of destruction and disaster (James 3:3-6). Jesus talked about a mustard seed. I'll be preaching about that Sunday.

Pay careful attention to the little things. If we look after the little things of life, the big things take care of themselves. Men don't trip on mountains, but we do stumble on stones.

Be careful when you write your checks this week — zeros stand for nothing unless they are in the wrong place. Satan always enjoys "spending" those misplaced little zeros.

See you at the place Sunday where God can "take a little and make a lot out of it"!

— John Ed

May 20, 1979

VALID IDENTIFICATION

Recently, the Los Angeles Police arrested a 33-year old woman who had swindled the county out of more than $48,000 in welfare payments, using 8 falsified driver's licenses over five years. Gil Mardilla, supervisor of technical services of the California Department of Motor Vehicles, said "A license is the most commonly accepted form of identification."

Jesus said that the most accepted form of identification of a Christian is that we "love one another." The fact that we are a member of the Church or use the name Christian isn't really the valid form of identification. He said, "By this ye shall know they are My disciples if they love one another."

False driver's licenses are easy to get. In New York a pornography ring obtained birth certificates of numerous children who had died in infancy and used them to obtain hundreds of illegal driver's licenses in New Jersey and New York. In Connecticut, a man forged 10 driver's licenses and sold them to teenagers to use for buying liquor. No statistics are available on the number of phony licenses, but a 1977 study by the California Department of Motor Vehicles found that it had issued licenses to 313,000 more men age 20 to 44 than the census had found living in the state! They also discovered that valid California licenses had been issued in the names of almost a thousand people who had been dead for years! The false identification for being a Christian is easy to obtain also — all you have to do is act your natural, sinful self.

Look alike licenses are also easy to obtain. One New Jersey policeman says all you have to do is walk in some shops on 32nd Street in Manhattan and you can get an official looking license that would be difficult for anyone but an expert to detect. A lot of people become good at imitating the Christian faith and even fooling a lot of folks, but the official look alike is not the real thing.

That false identification costs everybody involved. Arthur A. Trisch of the American Association of Motor Vehicle Administrators estimates that phony driver's licenses cost United States citizens about one billion dollars a year. False identification as Christians really is a high cost factor too — both in terms of all of the people who become turned off to the Gospel through counterfeit Christians and the financial loss through people who do not return the tithe to the storehouse of the Lord.

Being a Christian carries with it a big responsibility. Our basic identification is our allegiance to Jesus Christ and a lifestyle that demonstrates His way of life. Counterfeit identifications are easy to get, widespread, and cost everybody a lot.

See you at the place Sunday where we revalidate our licenses!

— John Ed

June 24, 1979

YOU ARE IMPORTANT!

One morning on the 6:00 a.m. devotional on WLWI, I made the point that God often puts us in a position to do something that perhaps nobody else would have the opportunity to do. I believe that. Oftentimes, there is something that I am in a position to do that nobody else will get that opportunity to do.

That same morning that I made that point on the devotional, one of our good members, D.P. Jones, was traveling to Anniston on a two-lane road through Elmore County. You might remember how there was a big accident between two tractor-trailer trucks in which people were severely injured and traffic was completely blocked on a bridge.

When D.P. got out of his car to examine the situation, he confronted a young man in the car just in front of him who was very frustrated. He was a soldier who had just flown into Mobile from England and had rented a car in order to be in Anniston for a court trial at 9:00. It was imperative that he be there, and he found himself caught in a traffic jam with no chance of making it to Anniston.

D.P. travels that area of the country often and knew of an alternate route that they could possibly take, utilizing back roads that you wouldn't find on a map. There was probably nobody else in that line of traffic who knew of the alternate route.

D.P. and the young man got their cars out of the line of traffic, followed the alternate route, and made it to Anniston just in time. Nobody else could have done it, — but D.P. was there and offered his help.

Everyday you and I meet people to whom we ought to make a positive witness for Jesus Christ. You might be the only person who is at the right place at the right time — don't miss the opportunity! God has something for you to do that nobody else can do as well as you.

See you at the place Sunday where we are always *training* to offer what we have at the right time!

— John Ed

July 15, 1979

LANDING AT THE WRONG AIRPORT

On August 1, 94 passengers boarded a Western Airline Boeing 747 in Denver and thought they were going to Sheridan, Wyoming. The pilots made a slight mistake and landed the big plane in Buffalo, Colorado. Nobody knows exactly what happened except that the pilots probably mistook Buffalo's small, well-lighted airport for the larger jet port at Sheridan. The whole incident is under investigation by the Federal Agencies.

When the pilot realized his mistake, he tried to turn around on the runway. The nose gear of the 103,600 pound jet sank through the asphalt. This incident ought to cause us to take a look at our lives and where we are going.

Now the pilots did not intentionally land at the wrong airport. For some reason they could not tell the airports apart, and all the modern, complex instruments on the plane did not help. You and I had better take a good look at the ways we spend our time, energy, and money. Are we investing in things that are real, or just appear to be real? It's easy to mistake the real for the artificial.

After this mistake, the people in Buffalo proclaimed Pilot Lowell Ferguson and his copilots, J. H. Bastiani and D. M. Webster, heros because they made the City of Buffalo famous by giving them national attention. Sometimes our mistakes might bring attention to us, but it is certainly not the kind of thing that we want to be remembered by. I don't want people remembering me for the things that I did wrong!

The flight is important, but where we land is crucial. If your flight plan ended today, where would you land and spend eternity? The Bible teaches that there are only 2 "landing places," and the wrong one has a wide runway and bright lights and can be easily mistaken. Better check carefully — the flight plan doesn't include the landing time!

See you at the place Sunday that will point you toward the right place to land!

— *John Ed*

August 19, 1979

YOU GET MORE THAN YOU ASK FOR

Two months ago in Pensacola, Florida, 37-year old Larry William Self appeared before Judge William Rowley in Escambia County Circuit Court to have his bond reduced in an auto theft case. Rowley obliged by reducing bond from $5,000 to $2,500.

As Self was leaving, he began cursing the jailers and the judge. When Judge Rowley inquired about the problem, Self replied with profanities and said, "If you ever want to tell me anything, mail it to me." Rowley responded by saying, "I won't have to mail you this - I am finding you in contempt of court and sending you to County Jail for one year."

"Why not make it five years," Self asked? "All right, you have got it," the Judge answered. "Why not make it ten years," Self asked? "You have got it - ten years in County Jail," Rowley said. Self then dared Rowley to raise his bond to $50,000. The Judge more than accommodated him by raising it to $100,000 and a ten year sentence for contempt of court!

When you ask God for something, be prepared to receive that - and more! The Bible says that you receive not, because you ask not. Jesus said, "Ask and it shall be given you, seek and you shall find, knock and it shall be opened unto you." God always gives more than we ask for. Many people in our congregation have recently experienced how abundantly God answers prayer.

Last Sunday, God blessed us with a great day as we had increases in every area — 826 in Sunday School, 1,361 in Morning Worship, 371 in Evening Worship, and people joining at all 4 Worship Services. And the blessings that aren't reflected in any kind of statistics were even greater!

This incident in Pensacola also reminds me that a temper can get you into trouble — Larry Self now has ten years to think about some ways to control his temper. Read James 3:2-12.

See you at the place Sunday where we will be asking for and receiving some big things!

— John Ed

September 23, 1979

INSTANT INTEREST

Our age might be characterized as the age of the instant. We are interested in instant coffee, instant food, instant printouts, instant credit, etc. Now I understand that a New York bank is offering "instant interest" on savings accounts in the form of appliances, vacation trips, cars, etc.

If you deposit $1,475 with them for two years, for example, you can "instantly" walk off with a 19" color television (instant on no doubt). Or if you deposit $160,000 with them for eight years, you can drive out with a Rolls Royce, instantly. I expect the instant interest wrinkle will be popular.

The Christian faith has the best to offer in an age of the instant. The central theme of the preaching of Jesus was that the Kingdom of God is now (Mark 1:15; Matt. 10:7). The people of His day misunderstood it because they thought it was something for the future, and Jesus had to constantly remind them that the Kingdom of God is now — it is at hand — it is among you. Heaven is not something you wait for at the end of your investment of faith, but is something you have immediately when you commit your life to Jesus Christ. Jesus said to the thief on the cross, "Today, you will be with me . . ." To the woman at the well who was looking for the Messiah in the future, He said that He was the Messiah and He offered her the water of life at that moment.

The instant interest from the banks in the form of appliances and cars will depreciate quickly. The Christian investment of faith is opposite — it appreciates each day. It is something in which we grow and develop, and its value increase each day.

At the end of the specified time, the bank gives back only your original deposit. The Christian investment gives the abundant life which appreciates each day, *plus* eternal life forever.

Christianity has so much to say to the age of the instant. What I am writing about here is no new gadget or gimmick to get people to invest themselves — it was spoken 2,000 years ago by the One who began His public ministry by saying, "Repent for the Kingdom of God is at hand."

See you at the real *instant interest* place Sunday!

— *John Ed*

October 14, 1979

A GOOD IDEA

Poor Father Edmond J. Nadolny — he is a Priest who heads up evangelization projects for Roman Catholics in and around Hartford, Connecticut. The Archdiocese did not budget enough money for him to do his work effectively in 1979, so he came up with a brilliant idea. He took out a personal loan of $20,000 and "loaned" the money to fifty screened applicants who would "multiply" the money for Christ and the work of evangelization in Connecticut.

It was a brilliant idea, except that Father Nadolny didn't realize that some people would forget it was a loan and just keep the money and use it for their own benefit. In short, his project turned out to be a phenomenal flop. Only five people returned any money leaving him with $18,000 to repay out of his own pocket.

Father Nadolny wrote that the people, "never used the money for the creative ideas they described, they used it for themselves." When he asked some of the people about the money, they made such comments as, "get off my back," "get lost," "maybe I'll pay you back someday." The saddest thing was the Priest said that the people were such creative "liars" that they seemed to convince themselves they had done nothing wrong.

Before we condemn the folks who mistreated Father Nadolny, I would ask each of us to check our own checkbook stubs for giving to Frazer. God has given us everything that we have, and the Bible clearly teaches from beginning to end that it is His idea that we return at least a tenth to Him. He has a right to expect fifty percent, or forty percent, or twenty percent, but He simply asks for ten percent as a beginning point. If my checkbook stubs don't show at least ten percent, I am more guilty with God's money than the people who were unfaithful with Father Nadolny's money (read Malachi 3:8-10).

We have both the opportunity and the responsibility for handling God's money. You'll hear some guilty people saying, "get off my back," (some will just think it — others may use stronger words). The saddest part is that some will work hard at "creative rationalization" to try and convince themselves that their idea is right.

God's idea is not only right for the evangelization of the world — it's right for me. My responsibility is to accept it and practice it!

See you at the place Sunday that has the *Best Idea!*

— John Ed
October 28, 1979

MINISTERIAL MALPRACTICE

It has finally happened — ministers are being sued for malpractice. It was not rare for lawsuits to be filed against ministers who served as trustees of institutions or sued as employers, but now the suits involve malpractice.

In the Chicago Tribune, Ann Keegan tells of a sick woman who tells her minister she is not getting better despite frequent visits to her doctor. The minister suggests that she get a second medical opinion. When she does the first doctor gets made and sues the minister.

Another lawsuit was filed against a minister because he counseled a woman to try a separation from her husband. The husband attacked the wife who separated from him, shooting her in his rage. The wife sued the minister for bad advice.

How many ministers does Frazer have — 3 or 2,075? The New Testament makes clear that every person who believes in Jesus Christ is a minister. The New Testament did not have our problem of separating ministers and layman. Ordination sets a minister apart for the purpose of administering the sacraments. The conduct of practice (or malpractice) of Christian living comes under the same standard of evaluation for all Christians.

Malpractice is probably the biggest problem confronting the Church. When looking at how well we practice the Christian faith, a lot of professing Christians might be guilty of malpractice — how many times are we willing to forgive, do we love all people, how well do we follow the Biblical guidelines of Christian living. . .?

Church Mutual Insurance Company is now offering a policy to protect ordained ministers from malpractice. The best insurance against malpractice facing all of us as ministers is a deeper commitment to Jesus Christ, a stronger obedience to His will for our lives, and a greater reliance on the Holy Spirit to give us power to do what we should do.

All 2,075 ministers of Frazer need to be aware of the malpractice suits. We ought to live our lives so that if anyone speaks evil of us, no one would believe them.

See you Sunday, at the *training* place to avoid malpractice!

— *John Ed*

November 25, 1979

CHRISTIANITY CAN CLEAR YOUR CONSCIENCE

Each Wednesday morning I go out to Southern Guaranty Insurance Company for a devotional with all their employees. Recently, they received the following letter that I want to share with you.

Dear Mr. Thompson,

I called you long distance on December 26 concerning an accident that happened about 15 years ago. A man insured by your company ran into the side of my car. The mechanic who repaired my car asked me if I wanted to replace the whole side panel and I said yes. But all that the mechanic did was to beat out the side panel and repaired the rear fender.

Your company was charged more than the cost of repairing my car. As well as I can remember, it was close to $200 too much.

Because of the grace and mercy of our Lord Jesus Christ to me I am able to return this $200. There are some things that I cannot straighten out, so I will just have to ask the Lord Jesus Christ to forgive me. But since the Lord has helped me to be financially able to return this money, I want to do so. Please accept this check and I am sorry about this.

Sincerely,

Christian conduct will clear your conscience. Do you have anything you need to "straighten out," like a letter of apology, confessing a wrongdoing, releasing God's tithe, repaying a debt, etc. . . .

See you at the *conscience-clearing* place Sunday!

— John Ed

March 2, 1980

PASSPORTS

One of the first things we had to do after deciding to go to the Holy Land was to secure a valid passport. Then we were instructed over and over again to always keep our passports with us because it was the only thing that would get us from one country to another. The passport became a priority.

The passport to the abundant life here and now and eternal life is the death/resurrection of Jesus Christ. It is the only valid passport into the Kingdom of God. That passport is essential before we can move from one state of growth to another.

Each person had to have his own passport. It was personal in the sense that it contained your picture, information pertaining to you, and no one else could use it. The death/resurrection event must also be personal with you. You can't get by on someone elses experience.

We had to keep our passport with us at all times as it was usually checked everyday. The Easter event is not just something that happens once a year, but is something that ought to express itself through our lives many times each day.

I noticed that each country we visited had a permanent place for checking passports. However, I noticed that several places had temporary facilities to accommodate unusually large groups. Since Easter is the largest attendance of the year, and since we would like to have the whole Frazer family together in one Worship Service, we are moving from our permanent place at Frazer to temporary quarters at the 4,000 seat AUM gym. I want to remind you that there will be a nursery at the Church beginning at 9:15 a.m. and it will be well staffed with nurses and adults. The AUM gym is less than 5 minutes from Frazer and there will be ample signs and ushers to direct you. There will be chairs on the floor for about 600 people and everyone else will sit in the bleachers. If people can sit in the bleachers for 2 hours for a basketball game, or a graduation event, etc., then a 1 hour Easter Service should not be unduly uncomfortable! We will have a 150 voice Choir.

Be sure you have the valid passport with you at all times. If you don't have the most important passport of all, I know where you can get a real one!

See you at the "temporary passport place" Sunday!

— *John Ed*

April 6, 1980

A BANK PRANK

Last week Dallas Cowboy's Defensive Back, Dennis Thurman, was arrested for an attempted bank holdup. He finally convinced officers that it was just a prank and they have decided not to press charges.

Thurman went in the bank with a friend to get a check cashed. He told police that he, "just got a little bored." About 1:30 p.m., he wrote the following note, "Dear Teller, this is a stick-up, please don't make any false moves or noise. I have a gun and I will use it. Signed, Robber." Thurman handed the note to the teller and asked her what she would do if someone handed her a note like this. Another employee saw what was happening and stepped on a silent alarm. The police quickly appeared and arrested him.

My first reaction to that news release was that it was really a stupid prank. Somebody could have easily been killed. How could anybody do anything as foolish as that?

A more serious prank many good people play is showing people a lifestyle (note) that indicates that God is not *first* in their lives. Many people play a prank on their friends by never witnessing to them about the real meaning of life. Some parents who are casual about Church attendance really trick their kids into believing that God and the worship of Him is not so important at all. Many Church folks play a prank on God each Sunday by giving less than He expects. These pranks, along with others, are pretty stupid because somebody will die and not realize what life is all about - or know about eternal life.

Thurman said that he would never try a prank like that again. Maybe a checkup on the "notes" that we are giving might show us how dangerous some of our pranks are. There is no place for dumb, dangerous pranks!

See you at the "no-prank" place Sunday!

— John Ed

April 27, 1980

WAS SHE A PHONY?

There was quite a dispute at the Boston Marathon last week. The female winner's medal was given to Rosie Ruiz who finished the 26 mile, 385 yard Boston Course in 2 hours, 31 minutes, and 56 seconds. This was 4 minutes better than the Woman's Record at Boston, and was 26 minutes better than Rosie's only other Marathon time in last October's New York Marathon where she finished 23rd among the women.

Immediately people became skeptical. Fred Lebow, President of the New York Road Runner Association, and others, labeled her a "phony." Not only was her time incredibly fast, but she didn't look tired enough, didn't perspire enough, didn't know enough about running terminology, and just generally didn't look like she had run a 2:31 Marathon. Some are suggesting she only ran the last 10 miles of the Marathon. Embarrassed officials are trying to figure out what to do with a possible phony.

Jesus was very concerned that his followers were not phony about their commitment. It is possible for a phony to put up a good front and fool some people, but Jesus always insisted that authentic Christianity is a life-changing experience that is expressed naturally through the person who is a new creation.

In Matthew 6, Jesus warned against phoniness when we pray, give, and fast (there's probably less phoniness in fasting since most folks have a tough time dieting, much less fasting). In Matthew 23, He denounces the phoniness of the Pharisees for appearing outwardly beautiful, but inwardly carrying the stinch of death. Pharisee phoniness is a tempting substitute for real religion!

There's no doubt in anyone's mind that Bill Rogers was the male winner of the Boston Marathon. There is a big question about Rosie Ruiz. How about you — do people know without question that your life demonstrates that you are seeking first the Kingdom of God, or are there areas that raise questions of doubt? Pharisee phoniness, like counterfeit money, will eventually be detected and leave somebody holding something that has no value.

See you at the "real" place Sunday!

— John Ed

May 4, 1980

TIGHTENING THE BELT

"Tightening the belt" is a phrase that we are hearing often from government and civic leaders during this period of high interest rates and inflation. Many suggestions are being made to help tighten the belt. Recently a person asked me, "Don't you feel that tightening the belt will mean that Church giving will be one of the first places people cut?"

Take a look at your belt. There is a front of the belt that comes through the buckle first. As you tighten the belt, the front part grows longer. The Bible teaches that everything comes from God, and the first of our fruits are to be returned to Him. The giving for God's work comes from the first, not the leftover. A Christian begins his personal or family budget with God's tithe, and arranges his other items in order of preference. A young couple shared with me last week a thrilling story of what tithing is doing for them as they are starting a new business.

So, belt tightening means that the first part becomes longer. The church composed of people following Biblical teaching and commited to the Christ of the Bible should have more funding to expand its programs!

Now I know there are a lot of people in the Church who would rather "play" at Christianity than be a Christian. They find logical "reasons" why they cannot return the tithe first (this was Adam's problem and subsequently ours). They view the Church as if it were some other club or group that can be placed anywhere on a list of priorities. They put personal interests first, and give from what is leftover. If the Church is composed of this type of commitment, tightening the belt will squeeze that Church out of business — and it deserves to die.

How will tightening the belt affect you — and consequently Frazer? I've got a feeling that Frazer folks will let belt tightening be our strength and not our squeeze! Oh, if belt tigthening is a problem suspenders are not the solution — but a restructuring of priorities is

See you at the "Belt tightening" place Sunday!

— John Ed

June 8, 1980

SAYING AND DOING

I overheard a group of older kids talking with some younger kids about starting to school last week. One of the younger kids is a fifth grader at a private school. The high schooler was asking about some of the requirements in the Bible Course for the fifth grade. The youngster replied, "We have to do the Ten Commandments," and then continued with several of the other requirements.

I was fascinated by that requirement of "Doing the Ten Commandments." I entered the conversation by asking, "What do you mean — do the Ten Commandments?" The youngster quickly replied, "Oh, we don't have to do them. We only have to be able to say them."

Now I know what he meant, but I am afraid what he said strikes at the heart of the ineffectiveness of the church today. Too many of us are content to say the Ten Commandments (and other Biblical principles) without doing them. I have one friend who jokingly says that he is looking for a church that requires you to keep only five of the commandments and do the best you can on the others. Doing the best you can was never a teaching of Jesus.

Doing is a lot more difficult than saying. The Bible teaches us that we are to be doers of the word and not hearers only (and not readers only!). How we walk communicates far more than how we talk.

This concept is so important to families. Parents who say that being a Christian is important, but do not attend church each Sunday, are preaching a sermon with their lifestyles that kids hear much more clearly than what was said. This Sunday marks the beginning of a new Church School year. It is an excellent time to put into practice the priority of expressing the Christian faith through Sunday School and Worship every Sunday.

Doing evangelism is more important than talking about it. I preached about this at the Jurisdictional Conference and several have suggested that I preach that sermon at Frazer. I will do that Sunday.

See you at the place Sunday where we are trying to make doing the same as saying!

— *John Ed*

September 7, 1980

67

RICH OR POOR

Mrs. Bertha Adams was a 71-year old widow who died recently of malnutrition in West Palm Beach, Florida. She often went to her neighbors and begged for food. She weighed only 50 lbs. when she died. One of her neighbors, Russell Blair, said, "Her house looked like a pig pen and she got what clothes she had from the Salvation Army."

But after her death, they have discovered that she had $800,000 in cash and at least $40,000 in stocks. Her lawyer, Robert Leite discovered her wealth when he found some safe-deposit box keys and opened the boxes. He says that he is continually flabbergasted and he just can't get over seeing that much money in cash.

It is a sad story. Here is a little lady who is almost a millionaire, yet living without enough food to eat or clothes to wear. She is now described as a "good businesswoman," but that description never benefited her.

So many people live like paupers when God has intended *life* with all of its fullness for us. Many people are living in big houses and fighting the "battle of the bulge," but dying of spiritual malnutrition. God wants to be our Father and provide more of everything that we need, yet Bertha Adams is being relived in so many people.

Jesus said, "I have come that you might have life, and have it more abundantly." That's God's gracious invitation to you and to me today. God has more resources for us to use than Bertha had stored away!

See you at the place Sunday that is "rich in God's Grace"!

— John Ed

October 12, 1980

CHRISTMAS — 1980

I received a Christmas card in the mail on Saturday morning. I did not recognize the name or the return address on the envelope, so I did not open it immediately. Later that afternoon I sat down at my desk and opened it. Boy, was I surprised!

When I took the card out of the envelope a twenty dollar bill fell out of the card. I opened it and found the following message:

"Dear Rev. Mathison,

> The enclosed money is for money I spent out of the
> treasury when I was treasurer of a class in your
> Church as a small child. I have now become a
> Christian and wanted to return the money. I ask
> you and your Church to forgive me of this sin as
> the Lord has forgiven me."

Wow! That's what Christmas is all about. Jesus Christ came into the world to change us from what we are to what He wants us to be. He came to point us to a new direction of life and a new lifestyle. He came that we might be forgiven — and forgiving. That card was the best one I received this Christmas.

I put the money in the New Building Fund. The new building will enable us to share this good news with more people so similar things can happen in their lives. What a way to build a building — using money from people whose lives have been changed!

See you at the "changing" place Sunday!

— *John Ed*

December 28, 1980

DON'T COMPLICATE THE DIRECTIONS

My Dad related to me recently an unusual and interesting experience in his life. He was visiting in a building in Panama City and stopped at a water fountain to get a drink of water. A sign above the fountain said, "Stoop and drink." He started looking for some button to push, lever to turn, or peddle to step on to cause the water to run. He was frustrated because he saw no means of starting the water to flow.

After thoroughly examining the water fountain and finding no obvious place to start the water flow, he asked for help. An observer said, "What does the sign say?" My Dad reread the sign, stooped to drink, and the water started to flow. It was controlled by a photo electric beam that a person breaks when he puts his head in a position to receive the water.

Sometimes we try to make Christianity too complicated. Jesus said, "Follow Me." Sometimes we try to add a lot of extras that a person has to assume before he can really be a disciple. We tend to add a lot of cultural trappings, or moralistic demands, or socially accepted practices to a person who wants to be a Christian. Paul faced that problem when some of the other Christians wanted to require some of the Jewish practices for a person becoming a Christian.

Jesus said, "Follow Me." That is all you need to do to receive the water of life that can quench your thirst forever. Quit looking for special buttons to push, or peddles to mash, or levers to turn. They will only hinder your following. Listen to what he says, "Follow Me."

See you at the "following" place Sunday!

— John Ed

February 1, 1981

DO YOU WIN IF YOU WIN?

In bold black print Northwest Airlines is promoting a contest with full-page advertisements which say, "Win a jet trip to Florida and take 2 friends along." The ad suggests, "Take your relatives, co-workers, church group, lodge, or neighbors." All contestants have to do is send in an entry blank. I was ready to enter and win and take the Administrative Board on the Boeing 727 to Ft. Lauderdale for 3 days and nights at a luxury hotel.

While the contest looks great on paper, someone has figured that the winner, if he makes use of the full value of the prize, is going to have about $50,000 added to his taxable income of 1981 and will probably lose money on the bill, even though the airline also is throwing in $15,000 cash. A tax expert estimates that a married couple with two children and a $25,000 income could wind up with an additional tax bill of $17,000, leaving them $2,000 in the red after using the airlines cash gift. If you make more than $25,000, your net loss would be significantly greater.

The first reading of an inviting invitation or advertisement can be misleading. Today you have to check the details to see if you are really a winner if you win.

So many different philosophies, gadgets, "cheap grace theologies," enticing advertisements, and other things are being thrown at us communicating that we will really win in life if we will buy what is being advertised — and a lot of people are falling for that. The Bible teaches that the road may be enticing and alluring, but in the end it can lead to destruction.

The best invitation I know was given by Jesus years ago — "Follow Me." You will be an ultimate winner in this life eternal if you follow Him. He brings no hidden agenda, no extra tax burdens, and no small print that will later trip you up. He just invites you to LIFE, and you can't lose with Him.

See you at the *winning* place Sunday!

— *John Ed*

February 8, 1981

A HEALTHY DISEASE

A little boy was going to quote the scripture from I Corinthians 13:13, "Now abideth faith, hope and love, but the greatest of these is love." When he stepped in front of the congregation and saw the huge crowd, he became a bit confused. He quoted the last part of that verse by saying, "But the greatest disease is love."

Love is a healthy disease. Jesus had an incurable case of it. He taught us that love is the distinguishing characteristic of being a Christian.

During the Valentine season the secular world places a big emphasis on love and makes it a multimillion dollar business of selling candy and cards. It is usually a shallow way of getting at the real meaning of love. Valentine is often only a symptom rather than the disease itself.

Love is a strange force. It changes enemies into friends. It is one unique thing that multiples by division — the more you give it away, the more you have. It is the one gift that grows bigger the more you take from it. It is one exercise in which it pays to be an absolute spendthrift. We discover that the more we give away today, the more we will have tomorrow.

The church family is one place where love is the most keenly felt and the most lavishly distributed. I want to preach about that kind of love this Sunday and pray that we might have an epidemic of it here at Frazer!

See you at the "healthy disease" place Sunday!

— *John Ed*

February 15, 1981

COMMON EXPERIENCE

Recently I met two men who are close friends. From my casual observation, I perceived that they had very little in common and couldn't really distinguish any similar interests. I was puzzled by their close friendship. Then someone told me that they both have kidney transplants, and that common experience has made them good friends.

I am often in the waiting room of the Intensive Care Units of one of the hospitals. I have noticed that various families form close bonds of friendship through the common experience of caring for someone in ICU. They are concerned about each other and each others families and support each other during this critical period. Sometimes those friendships last beyond the hospital experience.

The common experience that brings us together in the church is the saving grace of Jesus Christ. We have all had the common experience of the deathly sickness of sin, and have been exposed to the cure for our sickness through the grace of Jesus Christ. We don't have to have the same social or economic background, or even have the same special interests. The common experience that binds us together, not only as friends, but as brothers and sisters, is the "heart transplant" that God has given to us through His son Jesus Christ.

Paul reminds us, "You who were formerly far off have been brought near by the blood of Christ, for He . . . made both groups into one, and broke down the barrier of the dividing wall . . . So you are no longer strangers and aliens, but you are fellow citizens with the saints, and are of God's household." (Eph. 2:13, 19)

It is exciting to participate in and share the common experience of God's grace through the Frazer family. Every week brings different versions of that experience.

See you at the "common experience" place Sunday!

— John Ed

March 8, 1981

MIND SIGHT

Jason Thomas is in the 6th grade class at Charles Henderson, Jr. High School. He might not look like a hero, but he is in the eyes of everyone in his school.

Recently, he saved the life of one of his classmates. During lunch Gary Gillis choked on a piece of food, fell under the lunchroom table, and went into convulsions. Jason Thomas jumped to the floor and began hitting him across the back, an action that Troy Doctor Frank Robbins said saved Gillis' life.

Jason said that he knew how to react because he had read a poster several months ago in an office where his father works showing two examples of what to do if you saw someone choking. He said, "I read it one time months ago. I never thought about seeing the poster until I finished hitting him — then I saw it in my mind."

"Saw it in my mind" — one eleven-year old's casual reading of a poster while waiting for his father at work saved the life of a classmate. We must never underestimate the power and the importance of the little things we read and see each day. This is so true in the home. Most values are caught, not taught. Kids "read" something and might not think about it for awhile, but then a child can "see it in my mind" at the proper time.

Some plaques depicting Bible verses are good around the home, but lifestyles which depict the Biblical message are the most important signs. You never know how your reaction in a given situation might make an indelible impression on someone who is watching you.

See you at the place Sunday that's placing good things in front of people for them "to see it in my mind" later!

— *John Ed*

March 22, 1981

THE REAL ISSUE

Sunday before last everybody thought that Bobby Unser had won the Indianapolis 500. A rare event took place the next day when race officials took the win away from Unser for cheating and gave it to Mario Andretti.

When the yellow caution light is out at Indianapolis, a driver is not allowed to pass other cars. The video replay showed that Unser passed "eight or nine cars" according to Tom Binford, Chief Steward. Unser was therefore penalized one lap, giving the victory to Andretti. There were even accusations that Andretti had advanced his position during the yellow flag.

The sad part is that the issue was not so much that Unser had cheated as it was that he had been caught cheating. Andretti even said, "We all try to do this. A guy is smart for trying to do this." It seems that only those who get caught are considered to be outsmarting their opponents.

I was at the Federal Prison Camp recently — just visiting. There are politicians, respected business people, and some preachers there caught in "white collar" crimes. The general comment I heard was "a lot of people do it, but these people got caught." I hear young people say that "everybody cheats," as if that makes it right. Some married partners say that it is all right to be unfaithful to their spouse because "everybody does it." Some people operate on unethical business principles because "everybody does it."

Saying "everybody does it" does not make it right! Jesus never said, "Thou shalt not commit adultery — unless everybody is doing it." He did not say, "Thou shalt not steal, unless everybody is doing it." His principles for Christian living were never based on a survey of society. Even though 400 prophets of Baal said what the King wanted to hear, one prophet, Micaiah, spoke God's word (I Kings 22). Even though everybody else bowed down to Nebuchadnezzar's idol, three Hebrew boys refused (Daniel 3). David said, "I had rather be a doorkeeper in the house of my God than to dwell in the tents of wickedness" (Psalms 84:10).

Getting caught is not the real issue! Doing what is right is!

— *John Ed*

June 7, 1981

75

SEEING IS MORE THAN GOOD VISION

We recently hired a lady, Carol Wright, as our Financial Secretary. When she was interviewed for the job, one of the questions asked concerned her husband's employment. She stated that he was with Purolator Courier. Out of curiosity I asked some questions because I had never heard of Purolator Courier.

After the interview that morning I left the Church to visit the hospitals. At the first intersection I saw a truck at the red light with large letters PUROLATOR COURIER. Later, as I was leaving one of the hospitals, I saw a Purolator Courier van. The next day on the interstate I saw a large truck bearing the same name. That night I was watching television and saw a Purolator Courier commercial. All of a sudden it seemed that everywhere I looked I saw some representation of that company.

Now I know that I had seen some of the trucks before, but they had never registered. I am sure that I had watched some television program before that carried their commercial, but I never saw it. It wasn't until I met somebody with Purolator Courier that I even knew it existed and began to see evidence of its existence.

Something similar is happening in our Church with unchurched people in Montgomery. Our Work Area on Evangelism has held up before us the importance of being intentional about recognizing unchurched people and witnessing to them. I generally thought that most everybody had a Church — now I'm "seeing" that about half the people in Montgomery have no Church home. As we meet Him, we become more concerned about them!

Everyday you cross paths with at least 8 people who are unchurched. You see them everyday, but do you really see them? Take the time to say a good word for Jesus Christ and His Church. If you do not witness to them, who will?

See you at the "seeing" place Sunday!

— *John Ed*

June 28, 1981

76

A NEW VOICE?

If you are one of those people who gets upset when an elevator stops between floors, Otis Elevator may have the answer. Last month they unveiled a "voice", or a control system that gives a spoken message of reassurance.

In addition to giving reassurance when the elevator gets stuck, the "voice" announces floors through a sensitized speech to make elevator riding easier for handicapped. It also provides the time, weather, and even news on a visual display.

The whole system is the product of the latest market research. The "voice" has a basic vocabulary of 111 words and is the voice of a male. Psychiatrists reviewed the "voice" to obtain the most reassuring sound before selecting the lower tones of the male voice because they are more easily heard by people with hearing impairments. The color red was avoided on the buttons because color blind people have trouble distinguishing it.

Research has shown that over 50% of us have one phobia or another that is intensified when riding an elevator. This new verbal and visual information approach should help a great deal in reducing those fears.

Thousands of years ago God provided a "voice," not only to reassure us in dangerous situations, but to give direction in the everyday affairs of life. His word indicates that the people who hear and heed His voice find fulfillment and victory in facing all situations of life!

I don't know what market research He did on how to speak to people and visually lay out His handiwork of nature, but His track record is perfect! His "voice" always gives assurance, comfort, and direction for every situation of life.

See you at the "listening" place Sunday!

— John Ed

August 2, 1981

THE ROYAL FAMILY

Last week the eyes of the world were focused on St. Paul's Cathedral in London and the royal wedding of Prince Charles and Princess Diana. Three thousand people crowded into the Cathedral, along with Queen Elizabeth II, Presidents, royalty, and dignitaries from over fifty nations. Over a half-billion people watched on television.

The romance and wedding were like a fairy tale. Even though Lady Diana Spencer got Prince Charles' name confused as she repeated her vows, all rejoiced when they were announced as man and wife together.

I expect a lot of young people wished (and some even verbalized) that they could marry into a royal family. The fairy tale of meeting and marrying a Prince or Princess was relived in the minds of many people. I know of a girl who even told her mother that she wants her wedding to be just like that one!

The good news is that each of us can be a part of the world's finest royal family! The Bible teaches us that when we accept Christ as Saviour and Lord, we become a part of the royal family of the Kingdom of God. We become one of the King's kids. That is no dream or fairy tale, but a reality. Peter made it more special when he said that we are not just royal family members, but a royal priesthood! WOW!

The chances are slim for a person being born into or marrying into a royal family. The chances are abundant for a person to be *reborn* into the royal family of God. Being the King's kid is not left to chance, but decision. Only a few can be in the British royal family, but *anyone* can be in the royal family of God.

See you Sunday at the "royal family" reunion!

— *John Ed*

August 9, 1981

78

INPERSONATOR

Recently a member of the Orlando team of the American Football Association has admitted impersonating former Georgia All-American Guard Randy Johnson to obtain a spot on the team. Robert Lee Johnson told the Orlando Sentinel Star and television reporters that he used the similarity of names to enhance his chances of making the Orlando American roster, and then went along with the mistaken assumption made by others that he was the former Georgia and NFL lineman. He also listed the real Randy Johnson's high school, college, and NFL credentials on player information questionnaires and media interviews.

The real Randy Johnson now lives in Rome, Georgia, and was angered by the news of the impersonation. He said he might take legal action.

Coach Bob Williams became suspicious because Johnson did not seem to have the talent of a former All-American. His performance was poor. In fact he was not allowed to play in any exhibition game.

We go by the name Christian — that means little Christ or Christ-like. It means that our lives are to be an authentic witness to Jesus Christ. The world might consider some of us to be impersonators of that name.

We can give the proper credentials — church membership, sing in the choir, attend, give, etc., but the real test comes in our performance of how well we live the Christian faith. Who we are speaks louder than what we say about ourselves.

Like Robert Lee Johnson, impersonators become exposed sooner or later. While we might think it enhances our chance to make the Team to impersonate a Christian, the head Coach is never fooled. He doesn't get mad and threaten to sue the impersonator, but He genuinely rejoices and forgives when an impersonator repents and decides to be the real thing.

Genuine confession, commitment, and Christian living puts any person on the roster of the greatest Team of all — A Team that doesn't think of going on strike and a Team whose season never ends!

See you at the "Team" meeting place Sunday!

— *John Ed*

August 23, 1981

A WORLD OF "DIFFERENTS"

Jesus made a world of "differents" for me. The "difference" Chris makes in life is seen in the world of "differents" He gives to us.

Jesus offers a world of "differents." He does not take something an try to make it better or repair it. He gives something new. So man people miss the point of the Christian faith by just "trying to be a littl better." Jesus was not in the business of making people better, but c making people new!

One day He reminded us that we do not take a new patch and put i on an old garment, or else when it is washed it will shrink and tea away from the old garment. Rather, Jesus gives us a new garment. H also said that you cannot put new wine in old wineskins, because th old wineskins do not have the elasticity to expand with the fermentin of the new wine. They will burst. God doesn't put new life into the ol person, but he makes us new people!

Paul said that when a person is in Jesus Christ, he is a new creation Old things are passed away and all things become new Jesus is in the business of making us new and different.

He gives us a world of "differents" as we change from hatred to love from holding a grudge to forgiving, from being self-centered to being Christ-centered, from figuring how little we can give to how much we can give, etc. Christianity is a world of "differents." We have differen dispositions, different attitudes, different goals, different outlooks and most of all a different destination.

Jesus Christ invites each of us to the "differents" that he offers.

See you at the place Sunday that celebrates the "differents"!

— *John Ed*

September 27, 1981

BOUNDARIES FOR BALLS AND BEHAVIOR

The Toyota Tennis Classic was held in the Omni in Atlanta last month. It drew the top female tennis players in the world.

The tennis circuit plays on a portable court which is transported from city to city. As tournament director Larry King checked the court for the first match, he discovered that it had some wrinkles in it. The court was a Sporteze carpet and was improperly packaged for its flight from San Diego.

Just as the wrinkles were ironed out, WTA tour referee, Lee Jackson measured the court and found it 6 inches too long and 3 inches too wide (that's the kind of court I would like to play on). The tournament committee decided to pull the Sporteze court up and use a different surface which had the proper measurements.

The size of the court is very important in tennis — at any level. It is designed so that the game can be played within certain boundaries. Players practice on a uniform court and they expect each court to be the same.

The Christian faith has certain boundaries for our behavior. The Christian never has the option of "doing what I feel is right," when the Bible has a distinct directive for our behavior. To try to "stretch" those boundaries makes a farce of being a Christian. A major problem is that the weekend player (Christian and tennis) doesn't recognize when the court has been stretched!

It takes discipline and practice to keep a tennis ball inside the boundary lines, and it takes discipline and practice to live effectively the Christian faith. It might be easier to play on a "bigger court," but it's not the same game. Jesus said, "Not everyone who says unto me, Lord, Lord, will enter the Kingdom of Heaven, but he who *does* the will of My Father."

The time for Christian living is now. The first match is ready to start. Check your court. If it has been "stretched out" to the wrong dimensions, pull it up and get a new court!

See you at the place Sunday that's ironing out the wrinkles without stretching the court!

— John Ed

October 11, 1981

WEIGH-IN

Last fall, Montgomery hosted the World Championship Bass Master's Classic. Forty-two professional fishermen had qualified in regional tournaments and were here for the world championship. The event was covered by press reporters from across the United States.

The tournament was a three-day event. For a bass to be counted it had to be at least fourteen inches long. The fishermen left the dock every morning at seven o'clock and reported in at three o'clock for the weigh-in at the Civic Center.

I heard so much about the Classic that I went down on Friday afternoon to watch the weigh-in. I figured there would be just a few people there. Much to my surprise there were three thousand people present for the weigh-in!

I enjoyed listening to the talk of all pros and amateurs who had gathered for the big event. They were discussing various boats and tackle and lures and each had his own idea of the best place to fish and the best way to catch fish. Some were endorsing one brand of tackle over another. Each had his own idea of the best way to catch fish.

Ray Scott, the mastermind behind the Bass Anglers Association, was the master of ceremonies. In his own inimitable way, he entertained the crowd and kept them in suspense. He even told of one professional fisherman he saw giving one of his bass mouth-to-mouth resusitation to avoid a two ounce penalty if the fish died! Then, with all eyes focused on the scales, the total catch of 32 pounds made Stanley Mitchell the winner and $40,000 richer.

Jesus said, "Come after me and I'll make you fishers of men." In the final analysis it's not what style or form or place we use to witness, but how effective we are. We need less discussing and more doing. The good fisherman lets the weigh-in do the talking.

See you at the "weigh-in" place Sunday!

— *John Ed*

February 28, 1982

CLOSE DOESN'T COUNT

My family and I went to Washington D.C. for the AEA holidays. One of the highlights of the trip for Si and me was a visit to the Capitol Centre to see the Washington Bullets play the Phoenix Suns. I had met Coach John MacLeod of the Suns last Spring at the National Security Forum at Maxwell.

When we entered the Capitol Centre, I decided to buy a program. I then discovered that a special half time feature was a "shoot-out" sponsored by a camera company and an automobile dealer. Persons buying a program with a lucky number would shoot foul shots at half time, and the person making the most foul shots would have an opportunity for a shot from half court to win $1,000 worth of camera equipment and a new car. I was excited to discover that I'd bought one of the lucky programs and could participate.

It was a strange thing to walk on the court at half-time in street shoes and discover how far back they had moved the foul line since I played basketball! Ten thousand people watching didn't shorten the distance any. But I've always been able to shoot foul shots because those big guys don't guard you. I won the foul shooting contest.

I then moved to half-court. All I had to do was ring the basket and I would win the big prizes. I put up a beautiful long shot. I knew from the minute it left my hand that it was on dead center. As I was waiting for the net to swish, pictures of the new car were flashing through my mind. Even the crowd was quiet as they watched the ball descend. It was dead center - but about three inches short (a ministerial estimate).

I missed by just a little. I was lucky to have bought the right program. I was disappointed that I didn't perform to the extent that I could win the big prize. I'm grateful that God doesn't require us to be lucky before He chooses us to participate in His kingdom. The big prize is Life, the abundant and eternal Life that Jesus Christ brings, and our performance doesn't determine our winning that prize — it's a gift, it's His grace. The greatest prize of all doesn't require luck and it can't be earned. God gives it to each of us. But we must receive Him — close doesn't count.

See you at the "big prize" place Sunday!

— John Ed

March 21, 1982

WHAT DO YOU DO WITH ANNOYING SITUATIONS?

Earlier this month a predawn fire sent thick smoke through the Westchase Hilton Hotel in Houston, Texas, killing ten people and injuring thirty-five seriously. All of the people died of smoke inhalation.

Deputy Fire Chief Leonard Mikeska indicated that an employee, unaware of the blaze, cut off the hotel's alarm system because it's buzzing "annoyed" him. Some of the survivors said they heard a brief alarm for about ten seconds.

To shut off something that "annoys" can be disastrous. A lot of the passages of the Bible "annoy," so some people ignore them. A lot of people don't like to read about the *total* commitment that Jesus requires of His disciples (Luke 18:18f) - about the minimal standard of giving the tithe as genuine disciples (Matthew 23:23f) - the scathing denounciation of the religious leaders who say one thing and practice another (Matthew 23:3f) - the necessity of forgiving others before God forgives us (Matthew 6:14f), etc. Part of the meaning of Lent is that we set aside extra time to pay careful attention to all of God's alarm system that is striving to awaken us to some impending danger. Be alert to what the alarm signals mean in your life. Alarm systems are for responding — not cutting off!

One fire official said that the employee possibly did not know the meaning of the buzzer's ringing on the switchboard. It was out of ignorance that he unplugged the alarm. The church offers many avenues to educate the Frazer family through Sunday School, Bible groups, and a whole variety of ministries. If we "fail to know" we are not taking advantage of the opportunities offered us.

Someone has said that the ministry of the church is not just to comfort the afflicted, but to afflict the comfortable. God has a way of "annoying" us when He sees changes that need to be made in our lives.

See you at the "annoying" place Sunday!

— John Ed

March 28, 1982

84

TRUE OR FALSE

There is a new kind of moonshine roaming the Mississippi hills the Food and Drug Administration says, but instead of concocting white lightning, the bootleggers are cooking up fake maple syrup. They are producing thousands of gallons of syrup made of corn and cane but containing no maple. It is being labeled and sold as "pure maple syrup" in violation of Federal statutes, says Robert Fish, an FDA spokesman.

This makes the real maple syrup makers angry. "A bunch of renegades way out in the Mississippi boondocks are breaking the law, and the government seems unable to do anything about it," complained a spokesman for the American Maple Products Corp. It takes 35 gallons of sap to make a gallon of pure maple syrup, which retails for $27 a gallon. The new fake variety sells for about $16 a gallon Imitations and imposters have been a perennial problem for man. I have trouble distinguishing between the beautiful silk flower arrangements and live flowers. I have actually picked up false fruit from a dining room arrangement and was ready to eat it until I felt it. Counterfeit money is hard to detect.

Jesus had so much to say about the false and counterfeit. There were many religious people in His day who kept all of the laws, but they were fake. Jesus reminded us that talking and acting like a Christian was not the bottom line for entering the Kingdom of Heaven, but rather doing the will of God. He reminded us that trees might look good, but their existence is validated by the kind of fruit that they produce.

The best witness of the Christian faith is a genuine lifestyle that communicates the Good News of God's love. Quoting scripture and carrying a Bible is not as important as a lifestyle that demonstrates what the Bible teaches. The latest edition of the New Testament that many people will read will be your life.

I believe God is calling us to genuine, authentic Christian living. That which is real is lasting — the false will fade.

See you at the "real" place Sunday!

— *John Ed*

May 2, 1982

FRAZER BELL SYSTEM

As the Adult Handbell Choir played "Amazing Grace" last Sunday I thought about how much their presentation could teach us about discipleship and churchmanship. Those 11 people played a set of 52 precision tuned handbells, which meant that each person had at least two, and sometimes 3 or 4 more bells to play.

I was amazed at the coordination and unified effort of the 11 people. Each person rang precisely the right bell at precisely the right time. Joe Pat said that commitment is the first key to a good handbell choir. If one person fails to show, there is a silent spot each time that person's bells should be played. Commitment is the bottom line of Christian faith.

No one person in the choir could make music by ringing his bells alone. Each person's bell only contributed to the united effort of the whole choir. If some person decided to ring his bell at random, it would have been meaningless noise and chaos. The same is true in the church. Each of us has "a bell to ring" in the community of faith, and joined with the "bells" of others, the music of the Good News is played to the world.

A few bells ringing at the wrong time would have ruined the whole presentation. There is a specific time for each bell. That is so true of the church. The Frazer family is filled with multitalented people whose gifts and talents should be offered at the right time. It takes constant practice to put "the whole thing" together.

The bell choir takes seriously their ringing. They practice individually and as a group. There is nothing casual about their effort. Each day each of us has something to offer to the world in the name of Christ. We need to practice our faith every day both as individuals and as a church family. A bell choir nor a church needs ding-a-lings, but rather disciplined, practicing ringers!

I challenge you to upgrade the Frazer Bell System by practicing, praying, and working together that each of us might "ring our bells properly" in making the music that God desires for our church and our world. When He directs, and we follow, a mighty melody can come forth!

See you at the "ringing" place Sunday!

— *John Ed*

June 6, 1982

THE IMPORTANCE OF POWER

Recently I stopped by a place of business to speak to a man. I was greeted by the receptionist with these words, "I don't know who you are here to see, but he's not here." Then she explained that the power was off and everyone was taking an extended break. Some lady had wrapped her car around a telephone pole and knocked out the power for the whole area. She explained that a business can't do much work when you don't have any power.

I looked around the large room and she was right. The desks were empty and there was not the usual sound of typewriters, adding machines, and other office equipment. I looked at one new typewriter. It was a beautiful piece of machinery with all of the auxiliary parts. It had everything — except the power to make it work. The receptionist did tell me that the phones were working and they had called the power company and were assured that the power would be restored shortly.

A lot of people in life are paralyzed and rendered immobile by a lack of power. They have talent and ambition and necessary training, but can't seem to put it all together. They have good intentions, but never seem to get anything done. They spend a lot of time spinning the wheels of busy activity, but oftentimes meaningful productivity is not the end result. To such a person I would like to say that the lines are still open to the Source of power. He can quickly provide the power that gives a person a real purpose for living.

The parting words of Jesus to His disciples were, "You shall receive power when my Spirit comes upon you." That power is available to individuals in the church to help us utilize the gifts and talents that God has given us. I went back by the office that same afternoon after the power had been restored, and again it was buzzing with meaningful activity.

The power is on — plug into it! The power of Pentecost can cause our lives to produce the love and outreach God desires for Frazer.

See you at the "power" place Sunday!

— John Ed

June 13, 1982

87

DON'T STAND LONG IN ONE PLACE

I enjoyed watching them pour the foundation for our new Educational Building. The two-story building will be 17,000 square feet. The cement trucks kept pouring in the concrete. I discovered that they poured 325 tons, or 650,000 pounds of concrete. That is a lot of concrete!

I watched the men spread the concrete as it was poured into the foundation form. They were wearing those high boots and constantly moving while spreading the concrete. I made the comment to one of them that it seemed he always stayed on the move. He replied, "When you're spreading concrete, you have to move. If you stand in one place long, you might be there forever."

If you stand in one place long, you might be there forever. We know that's true concerning cement. I think it is also true in our Christian growth. The new Educational Building will be a facility to provide a means by which we do not stand still, but keep moving forward. It is a facility that will house growth opportunities. If we ever think we have arrived in our Christian growth, we can get cemented in and die where we are.

That principle is true in all of life. Where there is no growth, there is stagnation — and ultimately death. Growth is a necessary part of life. Growing in our Christian faith is like riding a bicycle — whenever you stop moving you fall.

Frazer offers a Sunday School class for every age group, and Bible studies throughout the week for our Christian growth. Don't stand long where you are — be part of a growth group and move forward!

See you at the "moving" place Sunday!

— John Ed

July 11, 1982

$1,000,000

One of our church members, Laura Milhous, received over $1,000,000 in the mail. That's right. It was more than $1,000,000 and she didn't expect it.

Laura is the owner and operator of Wicks 'N Sticks Candleshop in Eastdale Mall. One morning she received 25 boxes of candleholders from Britemetal Industries Corp. from Brooklyn, New York. The candleholders were wrapped in shredded American bills - twenties, fifties, and tens. It was more than $1,000,000, but shredded thin as cole slaw, and of no use to her.

The Federal Reserve Bank takes mutilated and worn currency from member banks and destroys it by shredding. Britemetal, Inc. buys 200 pound bales of shredded cash to pack it's product in. The cost is less than using regular paper.

Laura's "gift" created a lot of excitement at the Mall. She even got a visit from a Secret Service agent. Some people tried to put the bills back together, but found it an impossible task. All that money — and worth nothing.

What would you do if you received $1,000,000 in the mail? Since that is unlikely, a more important question is, what are you doing with the money you do have? The Bible teaches us that God has given us all that we have and He teaches us how to use it so it is worth something. How we use it is far more important than how much we have.

We can't take any of it with us when we die. Someone has well said that he never saw a funeral procession with a hearse pulling a U-Haul. Since we can't take it with us, and since how we use it helps determine where we go, we need a place like Frazer to teach us how to use what we have. That's taught here every Sunday!

See you Sunday at the place that's giving Something we can take with us!

— John Ed

July 18, 1982

NO SECRETS

The computer business is one of the most rapidly developing markets in industry. With advanced technology, the wide range of use of computers, and the ability to manufacture them more economically, it has become a booming business and a highly competitive market.

Since it is so competitive, each company tries to keep secret its research findings. Recently, we saw where IBM cooperated with the FBI to nab officials of Hitachi Ltd. and Mitushi Electric Corp. who were attempting to get IBM product manuals, code books, and computer parts. Charges were brought against 22 Japanese, American, and Iranian businessmen for allegedly trying to steal the computer information.

IBM has spent $7.9 billion on research in the past six years. That effort has generated thousands of bits of information that would be valuable to rivals in its highly competitive and technologically fast-moving computer business. IBM has always prided itself with its effort to keep secret what it finds. They use desk-checks, audits, codes and lawsuits, and even watch the trash bins. In that competitive computer business, employees are reminded that "Mum's the word." IBM is recognized for its ability to keep secrets.

The church has no secrets we're trying to keep. Churches aren't competitive with each other. We need to share what we know and learn from others. While many church people keep their relationship to Christ a secret, we need to go to the other extreme to share this Good News.

Research has shown that growing churches have many lay people sharing their faith daily. Witnessing is not the responsibility of the professional staff, but is the opportunity of each church member. That's the secret of Frazer's growth. We need to practice it continually and share it with others.

See you Sunday at the place that has no secrets!

— John Ed

July 25, 1982

SOMEBODY CARES

Michael Buchanan, a 17 year old youth, stood on the top of a New York hotel roof ready to commit suicide. The crowd below was urging the teenager to jump. A policeman, William Fox, told Michael that he cared about him and said, "I'd be proud to have a son like you."

Michael Buchanan, a 17-year old youth, stood on the top of a New who cared for him. The bachelor policeman became Buchanan's legal guardian and he moved in with Fox and his mother and entered a Staten Island high school.

Due to the publicity of the event, the mother he thought had abandoned him showed up and said that she cared about him. Gloria Hunsinger said that she had not abandoned her son 15 years before, but lost custody of him during divorce proceedings. She was told later that the boy had been killed in an accident. When the father mistreated Michael, he was shifted from foster family to foster family and finally wound up on a rooftop ready to commit suicide.

A boy's life was saved because somebody cared. And when that one person reached out to care, it opened up an avenue by which a young boy could be reunited with his mother. Today Michael is living with his mother, a brother, plus a half-brother and a stepfather. The family has been reunited.

There are many lonely people in the world. Each day we cross paths with many people who need to know that somebody cares. Most do not go to the brink of jumping off a hotel roof, but life for them is dull, drab and lonely. Jesus said, "Inasmuch as you did it unto one of the least of these . . . you did it unto me."

I have received several letters in the past few weeks from people who commented about the caring nature of the Frazer family. So many people have expressed gratitude over the way that people have reached out to them as a supportive, caring, redemptive community. I am grateful to be a part of such a caring group of people.

See you at the "caring" place Sunday!

— *John Ed*

August 29, 1982

UNEXPECTED BLESSING

About two years ago, I preached a sermon emphasizing how our disappointments can become God's appointments in life. We may be disappointed when one door closes, but God has a way of opening new doors to lead us in a different direction. In that sermon I used an illustration about a farmer who went through his first covered bridge. The farmer commented that the light in the opening at the other end of the bridge seemed so small when he entered, but the farther he went through the covered bridge, the larger the opening at the other end seemed.

At the invitation that Sunday morning, Bernice Howard came forward and rededicated her life. She became active in several aspects of the life of the church. She has become one of the faithful members of the choir. She personally has brought many people to Frazer to share in the fellowship that she has discovered here.

Three weeks ago, Bernice had major surgery in Huntsville, Alabama. When I visited her in that Huntsville hospital, she expressed her appreciation for the prayers of the Frazer family. When I commented about some of the cards that she had received from friends here at Frazer, she said that there were two special things that she brought with her to the hospital — one was her Bible, and the other was her favorite picture, which she had hanging on the wall. I looked at the picture and it was a covered bridge. She reminded me of that illustration and that morning when she rededicated her life. She said a friend gave her the beautiful picture of the covered bridge and it has become a symbol for her. As I looked more closely at the picture, I discovered that it had been painted by Ney Park, a member of our church. She could not believe that her favorite picture had been painted by a person in her church family!

That just reminded me how often we might bring unexpected blessings in the lives of other people without realizing it. Ney had just painted a picture, and I believe it was sold to somebody in Montgomery who gave it to someone in North Alabama, and eventually Bernice received it. Ney is a tremendous Christian, but I doubt he really thought that God would use his picture of a covered bridge to have such deep meaning in a fellow church member's life.

All that we do should be dedicated to His glory. Our talents, regardless of how large or small, can be greatly multiplied and extended by His grace. We never know what unexpected blessing one word, or one action, or one picture might be in another person's life.

See you at the "unexpected blessings" place Sunday!

— John Ed

October 10, 1982

A WINNING APPROACH

Those amazing Miami Dolphins - no one predicted that they would do very much this season but now they find themselves in the Super Bowl. They have marched right through their first three opponents in the Super Bowl Tournament.

I have been interested in the sport commentators' assessment of the Dolphin's success. There has been one dominant theme. They talk about how Coach Don Shula has evaluated the talents of his players, and built his system around their talents. Other coaches build a system and try to make the player's talents fit into the system. There's a big difference in philosophy there!

I hope here at Frazer we're trying to build the ministries of the church around the gifts and talents of our people. That's why we have a volunteer system. We ask every person to prayerfully consider what your gifts are and where God wants to use you, and then volunteer for that place. Since your gifts and talents determine the ministries of the church, it is important that each member volunteer to serve.

The ministries of the church are an outgrowth of the gifts of the people. We have spent the whole month of January training people for the places where they have volunteered. February 1st marks the beginning of our new year. If there is some additional area in which you would like to volunteer, or if you volunteered for some place and were not contacted, please inform us in the church office. We want every church member to be involved in the ministry where you feel that God is leading.

I like Coach Shula's approach. I believe that the church can win any contest in the world today when we allow God to direct us in employing the gifts He's given us in places of ministry. The Super Bowl in football is a small victory compared to what God is doing through His church!

I also like the Dolphins because the best man ever to wear a Dolphin uniform was Mike Kolen, and I appreciate what his witness means to my life, to Frazer, and to this city!

See you at the "winning" place Sunday!

— John Ed

January 30, 1983

DIALING THE RIGHT NUMBER

United Methodism has a toll-free telephone information service called Info-Serv in Nashville, Tennessee. Anybody can call them to ask a question and get an answer.

The February issue of the Interpreter inadvertently listed an old telephone number which was used by United Methodist Communications at 1525 McGavock Street, in Nashville, Tennessee. Since the agency moved the facility two years ago, the old number had been reassigned to a massage parlor. You can imagine the confusing answers that a Methodist pastor got when he called to inquire about some World Hunger resources!

If you don't dial the right number, you won't get the right answer. It's a good lesson for us. Jesus constantly confronted people who tried other ways, and His response was, "I am the Way, the Truth and the Life - no man comes to the Father but by Me." Trying to get an answer by making a survey of society will wind up a wrong number every time.

Last Sunday, one of the families who joined the church told me, "John Ed, part of the commitment of me and my family in joining this church is to pray for you, Joan, Vicki, and Si every day." I can't express to you how much their dialing that right number means to me and my family. I challenge you to pray for your Sunday School teacher, your leaders and every member of this staff every day.

The United Methodist Info-Serv number may change - God's number never changes. He is still the same seeking, loving, forgiving, empowering, challenging Father that He has always been. If your life is not in contact with Him today, it could be you're dialing the wrong number.

See you at the "right number" place Sunday!

— *John Ed*

February 27, 1983

IMPOSTER

His boss thought Dr. Jesse Adams was doing a good job as Tennessee's Director of Prison Medical Services and recommended him for a $4,000 raise. Actually, Dr. Adams was doing a better job of fooling people because authorities discovered that his real name was George E. Allen. When they charged him with practicing without a license and impersonating a physician, they discovered that his record went back to 1954 when he was sent to federal prison in Oklahoma for impersonating an Air Force officer.

George Allen had gotten his name, Dr. Jesse Adams, and his "identity" from a retired Naval Surgeon that he met in North Carolina. They became friends so George just decided to impersonate him. The people of Tennessee thought he was a real doctor because "he was very considerate of the program and was always quick to take defense of his doctors."

It seems that his wife was also pretty good at fooling people. She resigned her job with the Mental Health Department and told her supervisor she did not have the Duke University degree that she said that she did when she was hired as an accountant.

The word hypocrite literally means "imposter." It describes the way a person wears a mask during a play so that one character can play several characters by wearing different masks. Jesus had stinging words of denunciation for hypocrites.

One of the biggest problems facing the church today is people posing as imposters. More young people turn their back on Christianity because they see parents and adults who say one thing and do another. The Christian faith is advanced when real people live in a real world and make a valid, authentic witness of what Christ can do in a life.

It seems foolish that a person would try to impersonate a doctor - yet many people try to impersonate Christians everyday. A phony faith is repulsive. An authentic faith that is "the real thing" is contagious, winsome, and appealing to people.

See you at the "real" place Sunday!

— *John Ed*

March 13, 1983

THERMOMETERS AND THERMOSTATS

I oftentimes hear people confuse a thermometer with a thermostat. A thermometer is an instrument that simply registers what the temperature is. A thermostat is an instrument designed to regulate and change the temperature. The functions are quite different.

Sometimes as Christians we confuse our mission in life. We are never called simply to reflect the ideas and views of the world. We're in the business of changing the world. Paul warned us against, "Letting the world squeeze us into its mold" (Romans 12:2).

Thermostats and churches are always interesting. It is hard to regulate the temperature for every person. Almost every Sunday someone is fanning with a bulletin and someone else is putting on an extra wrap. I heard about a preacher who had different people "fiddling" with the thermostat, and nobody could be pleased. He finally just disconnected the thermostat and installed another one, hidden so it could not be found. People didn't know of the change and kept adjusting the old one. Everyone seemed happy, though there was no difference in the temperature!

The church should make a difference in the world. If we are "connected" to Him who can change things, then we fulfill our mission. If we're "disconnected," we are involved in a meaningless game.

I was in a church recently which had a large sign over the thermostat, "DO NOT CHANGE." It was an emphatic message for no one to fool with the thermostat. Maybe sometimes we put that kind of sign over our lives because we don't want God changing us too much. If a church ever hangs out a sign, "DO NOT CHANGE," it won't be a church very long.

See you at the "thermostat" place Sunday!

— John Ed

May 1, 1983

TEAM WORK

Last week Bill Bradley and Dave DeBusschere, teammates and roommates on the New York Knicks championship teams of the 1970's, were inducted into the Basketball Hall of Fame. It is the first time in history that two individuals from the same team, who played the same position, have been inducted together. Actually, four members, from the Knicks that won the 1971 and 1973 NBA Championships are now in the Hall of Fame.

I remember those Knicks teams. I was a great fan of theirs. The reason I pulled for them was that they didn't have as much size or talent, but they played as a team. DeBusschere said, "Other teams had more talent, we played together. The unselfishness and chemistry that developed between eight individuals that represented the Knicks was really something the people of New York could indentify with." Bill Bradley said that the teamwork of those Knicks teams was "as close to perfect experience as I could imagine in basketball."

Teamwork was the key. A lot of teams have great players, but the team that plays well together and is unselfish will be the one that ultimately wins. When I was in graduate school at Princeton, I participated with Bill Bradley in several Fellowship of Christian Athlete's programs and activities. He was always a "team man."

Teamwork is the key to the growth of the church. Frazer is a great team. One secret to growth has been the teamwork that has put together our various talents and contributions.

An integral part of the Frazer team is our elderly. Rev. Welton Gregory leads a super group of lay people in our Shut-In Ministry and our Ministry to the Elderly. This Sunday, we're going to be recognizing all of our members who are over 80 years old. The strength of Frazer is in large part due to the commitment, hard work, prayers, and team spirit of our elderly members.

See you at the "team" place Sunday!

— *John Ed*

May 15, 1983

A $24 RELIGION OR AN INVALUABLE FAITH

A Hispanic man who speaks little English walked into the DuBarry Pharmacy in Brooklyn and wanted to cash his lottery ticket for $24. When the clerk put the ticket in the computer terminal to verify that he had won $24, the clerk discovered that the man actually had a winning ticket worth 1.6 million dollars. When he tried to explain that to the Hispanic, the man got very upset and stalked angrily out of the store.

Some people pursued him and finally communicated to him what had happened. He was one of three persons who would split 4.8 million dollars. The man had a ticket that would provide him $79,000 for the next 20 years, but he almost did not understand.

The interesting thing is that one of the other winners has not even showed up to claim his prize. Officials were expressing concern that the person might not have known that he had won the large amount and might never cash the ticket. Somewhere there is a person carrying a ticket worth 1.6 million dollars.

As Christians we have something to share that is more important than 1.6 million dollars. Money can be unwisely spent or stolen, but the *Life* that Jesus Christ brings is something that no person can take away, and no money can buy. That life is available to every person, yet so many people walk around in this world without realizing that God has offered it to them. Life in all of its fullness is just a step away, yet so many people do not claim it.

Oftentimes the problem is communications. People who have received the life that Jesus Christ came to bring sometimes fail to communicate that to other people. Some folks just go to church and settle for a $24 religion when they could have a multimillion dollar faith! Some people stay frustrated and stalk around angrily because they don't understand all that God wants to give. What God has to give is worth far more than what man tries to buy.

The greatest gift in the world is available to you - if you claim it. You are already a winner of the greatest prize possible. Claim it — share it!

See you at the "winners" place Sunday!

— John Ed

July 17, 1983

THE REAL TRUTH ABOUT PHONY IMPOSTERS

Arthur Lee Trotter was really good at being a phony. He has been impersonating pro-football player Marv Fleming for years. He was so good at his masquerade that he even got one town to honor him at a "Marv Fleming Day!"

Police have discovered that Trotter has been impersonating people for almost 30 years. They found in the trunk of his car books with Fleming's name on them, pictures of Miami Dolphin and Green Bay Packer jerseys with Fleming's name and number, and even three insurance policies made out to Fleming listing occupation as a professional football player. There was even a newspaper clipping, complete with picture of Trotter and his girl friend, taken during the "Marv Fleming Day" celebration in Texas in 1978.

The sad thing is that Trotter now thinks he really is Marv Fleming. When the police told him he could quit playing his game and showed him the evidence, he looked at them and said, "That's wrong. I'm Marv Fleming."

Part of the problem of playing the game of being a Christian is that after awhile some folks begin to believe that it's true. Jesus was constantly shocking the phony religious people of His day because He wanted to call people to an authentic Christian experience. There's no place for playing the game of impersonation in God's Kingdom.

We are now beginning our commitment program for this year with the theme, "In His Steps." This is a time when each church member will commit himself/herself to serve someplace in the church in 1984 and make a financial commitment. The theme indicates that we should follow the steps of Jesus Christ in committing our time, talent and treasure to Him through His church. Phony imposters will look for a way to get by with as little as possible - people with a real faith will sincerely try to walk "In His Steps."

See you at the "real" place Sunday!

— John Ed

October 2, 1983

ADOPTION — FAD OR FAITH?

Adoption dolls - those little soft-faced cuties that require an oath of adoption and signed adoption papers accompanied by a promise of a good home, have been popular, but out of reach for most parents. Some of them cost up to $200 for a single doll. Now parents are literally beating down the doors of toy stores to buy these little darlings for their little darlings.

Coleco Industries developed the Cabbage Patch children. They plan to produce 1.4 million of them, and they sell at prices ranging from $18 to $25. These one-of-a-kind dolls, designed by computer come with birth certificates, disposable diapers, and detailed fingers and toes.

Over four million orders for the dolls have come in! The demand greatly outstrips the supply. One disc jockey in Milwaukee jokingly said that fifteen hundred of the dolls would be dropped by a B-29 bomber, and people flocked to the Milwaukee County Stadium to get their dolls. Shoppers have been injured in stampedes in toy stores. Some people have flown to London to get one (I assume citizenship papers come with them). One salesman in Montgomery has said that when the dolls arrive here, an ad will be run in the paper and shoppers will gather in the parking lot and numbers will be given to shoppers and the dolls will be given according to numerical order as long as they last.

One family is quoted as saying, "We can't have Christmas without a Cabbage Patch Kid at our house." Another has said, "My kid's Christmas will be ruined if she does not get a Cabbage Patch doll."

There is a far more important Child who is the real meaning of Christmas. Kids can go a whole lifetime without a Cabbage Patch Kid, but nobody can live without the Child who was born in Bethlehem. You don't have to stand in line in a parking lot, nor will you see Him dropped from a B-29 bomber, but He is available to every person. We can be His by "adoption." He is "One-of-a-kind," and He is for real.

I hope the real craze this Christmas will be toward the Babe who was born in Bethlehem. He isn't a passing fad - He is what Christmas is all about. If you miss Him, it will ruin your Christmas.

See you at the "real Baby" place Sunday!

— John Ed

December 11, 1983

A PAPAL PARDON AND PERSONAL PRACTICE

Last week Pope John Paul II met in a prison cell in Rome with Mehmet Ali Agea to express again his forgiveness to Mehmet. Over two years ago, the Turkish terrorist tried unsuccessfully to assassinate Pope John Paul. After the attempted assassination, Pope John Paul expressed forgiveness for his would-be assassin.

This meeting took place in Rebibbia prison. After visiting with Agea, Pope Paul said, "Today I am able to meet my assailant and repeat the pardon that I expressed immediately for him and was later to declare publicly when I was able from the hospital." Pope John Paul said that the meeting was "providential," it was neither planned nor programmed, but that the Lord gave them the grace to be able to meet each other as men and as brothers.

Forgiveness is essential to the Christian faith. Each of us has had someone to do something wrong to us. We have two options - we can either harbor a grudge and look for an opportunity to get back at them, or we can forgive them. Pope John Paul gave high visibility last week to an important practice in which every Christian must be engaged.

The Bible teaches us that our forgiveness of other people serves as a guideline for God's forgiveness of us. Mark 11:26 says, "But if you do not forgive your fellowman, neither will your Father which is in Heaven forgive your trespasses."

Forgiveness is essential not only to our spiritual health but to our mental and physical health. Medical authorities have indicated that so many physical symptoms result from unresolved conflicts and relationships. To hold a grudge or resentment ultimately destroys the holder.

Thank you, Pope John Paul, for setting a good example for what God's Word teaches and what we as His children are to practice. The Papal pardon is a guide for personal practice.

See you at the "forgiving" place Sunday!

— John Ed

January 8, 1984

EVERYDAY CHRISTIAN

In the City of Columbia, South Carolina there is a man who makes his rounds through the downtown streets and suburbs visiting people and trying to meet their needs. He calls on the elderly, the blind, the retarded, the eccentric, the forgotten. He brings food when the refrigerator is empty, rent money when eviction is near, and good times when a life seems choked with bad.

John Fling, 62, does not work for any organization. He just reaches out to people because as he says, "the scriptures say you look out after your neighbors." He gives away most of the small salary he makes from delivering auto parts for a Chevrolet dealership. He and his wife have no telephone, no television, and no car.

John visits a lady who is in need of food. He reluctantly accepts her $15 as he goes to the grocery store. Later he returns and hands her two bags of groceries. The receipt reading $32.35 is crumpled in his pocket. He presses $1.00 in change into her hand. People have discovered that it is not uncommon for Fling to take out a loan from his employers to tide over a landlord threatening to evict a jobless mother and her five children. The three cars he has owned in the last ten years have all been given to people who needed them worse than he did.

People affectionately call him, "Everyday Santa." He wears a cap that says, "I love to tell the story," and he tells it by what he does!

About the best title a person could go by would be "Everyday Christian." That term indicates that we put our Christianity into practice in everyday situations of life. Sermons that are seen last a lot longer than sermons that are heard!

In a city of over 100,000 people, John Fling is a rare exception - May God increase his tribe!

See you Sunday at the training place for Everyday Christians!

— *John Ed*

June 3, 198

DELIVER THE MESSAGE

There has been a lot of publicity given lately to the carrying of the Olympic Torch across the United States to light the flame signaling the start of the Olympic Games. There was a special ceremony at the White House, and from there dignitaries have been invited to carry the torch a portion of the way. Eventually it will reach Los Angeles.

The carrying of the torch has a rich heritage. One of the most gruelling events of the Olympic Games is the 26-mile marathon race. This race has a historic counterpart. In 490 B.C. the Greek Army under Miltiades defeated a large Persian Army at Marathon, about 26 miles from Athens. It was one of the decisive battles of history, and the whole existence of the State of Athens and democracy, as we know it, was at stake. A runner, Pheidipides, ran all the way to Athens carrying the news. Just as he arrived, he gasped out the word, "victory" and then dropped dead. He delivered the message!

The carrying of the torch and the lighting of the flame represents the message of the Olympics. It is both a ritual with historical significance, and a symbol of the beginning of competition for the coveted gold, silver, and bronze medals.

I once saw a cartoon which showed a runner with a torch coming swiftly to a group of anxiously awaiting Athenians. The runner arrived and just before he fell over, he gasped, "I forgot the message."

We Christians have a great message to carry. Sometimes we might be more like the runner who forgot the message, or remain silent about it. The most important game in town this summer is not the Olympic Games in Los Angeles, but the Game of Life. You might be carrying the torch to help light that flame! Be sure to deliver the message wherever you are. Pass the flame to someone this week with an invitation to church.

Vacation Bible School is June 25-29, and July is going to be Camp Meeting Month. These are means that God is going to use through the Frazer Family to carry the flame and deliver the message.

See you at the "message delivering" place Sunday!

— *John Ed*

June 24, 1984

VICTORY'S NARROW MARGIN

In the Olympics Connie Carpenter-Phinney won the Gold Medal in the Olympics Cycling Road Race. It was the first medal for the U.S. in cycling since 1912.

Now the amazing thing about her victory was that she won by the width of a bicycle tire. She rode that bike for 49 miles. She had been on it for two hours and eleven minutes and fourteen seconds, and after that distance and time the difference in winning was the mere width of a bicycle tire!

Oftentimes the difference in winning or losing is such a narrow margin. Connie has always been a competitor as she competed in the 1976 Winter Olympics as a speed skater and has won 11 National Titles as a woman cyclist. She saved the best effort until the end of that race to win by inches.

Too often in our Christian faith we are not persistent enough. We quit before the job is finished. We get discouraged or disappointed or despondent, and defeat easily becomes an alternative. Jesus spoke firmly about the importance of a second effort and going the second mile. Paul finished his life by saying, "I have fought a good fight, I have *finished* the course."

Don't every give up on some project that God has given you. Don't ever consider any person impossible when you try to share the Christian faith with them. If God called you to a task, give it your best shot; even to the end. Usually the difference in winning and losing is such a narrow margin.

Sixty thousand people watched that race. It was won by a few inches. More people than that are watching you and me in the most important race there is - the game of life. The writer of the Book of Hebrews even says, "We are surrounded by a Heavenly crowd of spectators." People are pulling for you. Remember - you and God always make a majority.

See you at the "winning" place Sunday!

— *John Ed*

August 19, 1984

LIVE CHURCHES — DEAD CHURCHES

There are two kinds of churches in the world today - live churches and dead churches. There is a lot being written today about the differences in the two. I would like to share some of these contrasts that I have heard, plus add a few of my own.

Live churches have lots of noisy youth and children —
   Dead churches are relatively quiet.
Live churches are planning for the future —
   Dead churches are reliving the past.
Live churches focus on people —
   Dead churches focus on programs.
Live churches present an unchanging Christ in forms of ministry that are changing —
   Dead churches do things the way they have always been done.
Live churches are filled with tithers —
   Dead churches are filled with tippers.
Live churches are friendly and receptive to newcomers —
   Dead churches wonder why they have no visitors.
Live churches focus on What's right with the church —
   Dead churches look for what's wrong with the church.
Live churches design worship in which the worshippers are participants —
   Dead churches have worshippers who are spectators.
Live churches have worship that celebrates —
   Dead churches have worship that is endured.
Live churches support missions heavily —
   Dead churches keep the money at home.
Live churches dream of God's dreams —
   Dead churches relive nightmares.
Live churches have music designed for the congregation —
   Dead churches have music designed for the musicians.
Live churches focus on Power —
   Dead churches focus on problems.

See you at the "Live" place Sunday!

— *John Ed*

September 30, 1984

HOW DOES IT LOOK TO YOU?

A CBS promotional ad last month in the *New York Times* pictured John McEnroe playing tennis right-handed. A spokesman for CBS blamed the mistake on the engraver's "artistic judgement." According to the embarrassed spokesman, the fellow flipped the photo because he thought it looked better that way.

What looks better and what is right is oftentimes two different things. One of the problems today is that people settle for that which looks better. The photo of John McEnroe might look better showing him playing right-handed, but that's not the way he has become the Number One player in the world. In fact, I would play him a challenge match for any amount of money if he played right-handed!

Sometimes it might be easier for a businessman to show a bottom line that looks better if he is willing to do a few things that are wrong. Sometimes students might be tempted to bring home a grade that looks better, even if it means cheating. Maybe an inferior product can be dressed up to "look better," but it is still faulty and not right. That which looks better is not better than that which is right!

That is the reason our Steering Committee has selected In His Steps as our theme for our Every Member Commitment campaign this fall. I know of no better theme that points us in the direction of what's right, rather than what might look better, than for each of us to be challenged to walk In His Steps as we make commitments of our time, talents and treasure. You can't walk In His Steps if you are willing to compromise to make it look better. The In His Steps calendar is included in this bulletin. Post it in a conspicious place in your home and pray for each event as the Frazer Family walks In His Steps.

As CBS is embarrassed over the promotional ad, so ultimately our ways will find us out. We might think we can get away with something for a while, but ultimately that which is right will prevail. What we plant is what we are going to reap!

See you at the "right" place Sunday!

— *John Ed*

October 7, 1984

SEE THE SIGN?

Last week I was watching the World Series. Joe Garigiola was the announcer. There was a runner on first base. As the pitcher wound up, Joe Garigiola said, "It's a pitchout." Sure enough it was a pitchout. The other announcers were amazed and wondered how he could call the pitch. He said it was simple - the Detroit Tigers were using the same signs that he had used as a catcher 25 years before!

The other announcers could not believe it. The Tigers were still using those same signs. A closed fist was a pitchout. One finger was a fast ball, two fingers signaled a curve, and three fingers fluttering called for a change-up.

The signs for a vibrant church are the same today as they have been in the past. One sign is that we are winning people to Jesus Christ. The last command of Jesus was to go into the world and share the Good News. The last command of Jesus should be the first concern of the church today! That sign hasn't changed at all.

Another sign is that people obey God's Word through tithing. Jesus spoke more about money than He did any other single subject. The first tenth of all that comes to me or any of us is to be returned to His storehouse. As Larry Burkett said, "That is an external sign of an internal experience."

Another sign of a vibrant church is that the people love each other. Jesus said, "By this you shall know they are My disciples if they have love for one another." Churches that lavishly and liberally distribute their love find that love is always splendidly replenished.

Are these signs evident in your life? Do you tithe each month? Have you won someone to Christ and the church in the past days? Are you building bridges instead of walls? The signs are still the same. The execution of those signs produce winners. Look what happened to the Detroit Tigers!

See you at the "sign" place Sunday!

— John Ed

October 21, 1984

A SIMPLE INVITATION

The phone call came on Friday afternoon. It was long distance. A lady's charming voice said, "I want to thank you and the people of Frazer Memorial because through your church the eternal destiny of me and my husband was changed." Wow! That is some way to start a conversation.

She went on to share how she and her husband were eating in a restaurant about a year ago. A gentleman and his family were seated at the table next to them. They politely spoke, and then the man engaged her and her husband in a moment of conversation. He inquired where they went to church, and they admitted that they had not been to church in years. He invited them to Frazer Memorial United Methodist Church.

The lady said that she and her husband attended, somewhat out of curiosity, but felt something in that service of worship that they had never felt before. They continued to come for a few Sundays, and in the privacy of their home made a commitment to Jesus Christ. They were transferred at that time, and they have become active in a Church in a different state.

She kept saying "That man's simple invitation changed our eternal destiny." Think about that - one little invitation that changed an eternal destiny. Eternal is a long time - in fact, it is forever. She kept offering thanks for that invitation of that man.

She did not remember the man's name or his family, but she said, "I'll never forget the warmth and compassion in his face when he invited us to Frazer." She went on to say that she had never felt the presence of God so strongly as the few Sundays they attended here at Frazer. Her telephone call was just an effort to say a tangible "thank you" for a church family that made a difference in their lives. In this way I pass on her gratitude to you.

One simple invitation. What did you talk about the last time you went out to dinner? What do you talk about at the office, in the grocery line, or when you are taking a coffee break? You cross paths with at least five unchurched people every day. Almost half of the people in the Montgomery area are unchurched. Have you ever stopped to think what one little invitation might mean - it could make an eternal difference in somebody's life.

Eighty-five percent of the people who joined Frazer last year came because someone offered a simple invitation. I am grateful for a church that is reaching out to a community. I am also convicted of the fact that each of us needs to be making that simple invitation more often. You have an opportunity to make it every day.

See you at the "invitation" place Sunday!

— John Ed

December 2, 1984

TRADITION VS. REALITY

The regular tickets for the National Hockey League's home games by the New York Rangers carry the term "NHL Championship" on each ticket. They are the only team among the NHL's 21 teams that refer to each game as "NHL Championship."

That's really strange because the Rangers last won the Stanley Cup in 1940, and they might even be resting on laurels that are older than that. Jack Fitzpatrick, senior vice-president of Madison Square Garden Corp., the Gulf & Western subsidiary that owns the team, says he has a ticket in his office from 1938 that bears that same inscription, "NHL Championship." He suggests that the usage could date from the Rangers NHL title in 1927, or even earlier.

Fitzpatrick justifies retaining the words "NHL Championship" by noting that league bylaws refer to the regular season's schedule of "championship games," but this doesn't explain why the words also appear in the 1984 preseason tickets. Everybody has explained it by saying that it is simply a tradition - a very, very, very old tradition.

If you go to see a New York Ranger's hockey game, you don't have the sense that you are watching a "championship game." If they haven't won a championship in 50 years, all the tradition of printing that on the tickets doesn't bring it to reality.

Christmas can either be a very, very old tradition, or it can be fresh and alive as you sense the presence of Jesus Christ in your life. The celebration of Christmas can be hollow or hallowed. Simply to label a day Christmas does not mean that we will experience the joy of "championship living" as Jesus can offer it.

I hope that each day you are experiencing victories in your life as you grow in the Christmas faith. The most important game in town is not being played on an ice rink, or basketball floor, or a football field - it's the way you live every day! It doesn't matter what you write on the ticket for your life, what does matter is Who is in charge of your life. All of the trimmings of Christmas cannot make the tradition of Christmas real - only Jesus Christ can do that. Tradition can never measure up to the experience of current championship living with Him who gives victory in all things.

See you at the "championship" place Sunday!

— *John Ed*

December 9, 1984

WHEN WALKING DOES THE TALKING

Recently a very successful businessman in another state shared with me why he hired the young lady to head up his marketing department. There were several applicants for the position who had advanced training and a good track record in experience.

One young lady, who is a member of the Frazer family, applied for the position. She did not have the training nor the experience of some of the other applicants, but she was hired for the job. The businessman said that the deciding factor was his concern how the person in this position would represent his company. He wanted someone with high standards. When he interviewed the young lady from Frazer, she simply told him that she was a Christian and would not do anything to embarrass her Lord or his company! He selected her immediately!

Since hiring her he said that she is far more capable and productive than he ever expected. When he found out about her home church, he shared the incident with me.

I am proud to be a part of a church that is training young people that how to live is more important than how to make a living! People who know how to live the Christian faith effectively make their Christian witness through the quality of their work. I just believe that more and more employers are looking for people who won't embarrass the company. If a person doesn't embarrass his/her Lord, they won't embarrass the company!

It is exciting to see the kind of Christian foundations that are being taught in Sunday School in our Children and Youth Divisions. Our College, Singles, and Adult groups are studying closely God's Word to determine personal response to ethical issues.

I believe that the biggest question the world is asking the church today is "Do you walk like you talk?" People are not so interested in what we have to say, but they are extremely interested in how we live. Your actions on the job each day preach sidewalk sermons that are the most effective. Practiced preaching is the most productive!

I am thankful for a church whose influence is making a difference in business in another state!

See you at the "walking" place Sunday!

— John Ed

February 17, 1985

PICK THE PROPER PLAN

Recently a funeral home in Florida advertised a new innovation in burial services. For about $4,000 they will cremate your body, put it into a small rocket and fire it into orbit. It is guaranteed to circle the earth for twenty-three hundred years. God has a better plan that is guaranteed forever.

Part of the selling pitch seems to imply that this is one sure way to get "up there." The problem is that Heaven is not necessarily "up there." Heaven is where God is, and He is certainly beyond any kind of orbiting rocket. Jesus said that the Kingdom of Heaven is here - it is within you. The only sure way to heaven is through Jesus.

I also wonder if part of the selling point might be that your friends can go out on a clear night and look up and see you go by. I suppose you could, for a little extra money, get some specialized, identifying lights so that friends would be sure that they have identified the right rocket. God's plan says that you can spend eternity *with* your friends!

I am also troubled a bit about the implication that you have to have almost $4,000 to be able to participate. The Bible teaches us that you don't have to have anything to participate in God's plan - just receive the gift of God's Son to you. Actually, it will cost you everything that you have. On one hand it is totally free to you - on the other hand you have to give up everything to have it.

I do have some friends that would feel right at home in that program of orbiting the earth after their death, because they spend most of their lives going around in circles anyway. That would seem awfully monotonous to me. I want to spend eternity where God is and a place where I think the Bible hints that there might even be a possibility of my singing a solo and sounding good!

Frazer is advertising the best plan I know because it comes from Him who created life and conquered death. You can be a part of God's Plan now. It is for any person who will simply accept and receive and follow Jesus Christ.

See you at the "Proper Plan" place Sunday!

— *John Ed*

March 3, 1985

111

TRAVELERS DON'T TAKE TREADMILLS

Recently I was in Coach Larry Chapman's office at Auburn University at Montgomery. He is the head basketball coach and I was trying to give him a little advice on coaching. I had a couple of good plays I had worked out for his team, but he didn't seem to be too interested.

He carried me upstairs and asked me to try out the new treadmill that they have. He said it was excellent for jogging. I put on my jogging clothes and thought I would give it a try. He put me on the treadmill running at six miles per hour. He set the clock for 45 minutes and walked out the door. When you are jogging on that thing, you can't quit. I expected him to come back, but he forgot about me.

Four and one-half miles and 45 minutes later, I was almost exhausted. After running that long, I figured I would step off somewhere downtown! But when I got off I was right where I had started. I had spent all that energy running, but had not gone anywhere. For some people, life is like that. They spend an awful lot of time and money and energy but never go anywhere. Life seems to be just a merry-go-round of meaningless activity. They run hard, but get nowhere. They get into a rut, and about the only difference between a rut and a grave is the difference in the depth of the two.

Jesus said that the Kingdom of God is "like a man traveling." Life is going some-where. Paul speaks of the "high calling of God in Jesus Christ" for each of us. There is purpose to what we are doing each day. Travelers don't take treadmills!

God has a plan and a purpose for your life. He wants to use you and your talents and energy and resources for something that He has designed for you. He wants to take you from where you are to where He wants you to be. And, that trip is filled with meaning and purpose!

Life is monotonous and boring if it is lived on a treadmill. Life is exciting and meaningful when people find themselves in the center of God's purpose for their lives. When you get where you are going, where will you be?

See you at the "traveling" place Sunday!

— *John Ed*

March 10, 198

HUGGERS

Recently I attended the Special Olympics Swim Meet at the Montgomery Therapeutic Center to give the invocation for the young people and adults from across the state who participated. It is a marvelous program for Alabama's special people.

As I entered the pool area, one of our beautiful college girls, Jill Miller, ran up and hugged my neck. She said she was happy to see my name on the program and I asked her why she was there? She enthusiastically replied "I am a hugger, every person who participates in any event gets a hug." There were a lot of other young people there as "huggers."

I watched these special people compete. Some of them weren't able to swim very far, but as each person got out of the pool they got a big hug for their effort. You know - our world needs a lot more huggers. Most of us respond more quickly to encouragement and affirmation than we do to put-downs and intimidation. I understand the church to be a place where people affirm, encourage, and support each other - hugging. People who experience hugs usually don't experiment with drugs.

In today's world we place so much emphasis on winning that we overlook people who are doing their best. The reward of personal satisfaction doesn't always go to the best but to the one who does his best. Have you given a "hug" lately to someone who simply participated and did his best?

Let me remind you that our morning worship service is now on WLWI AM which is 7400 on the AM dial. It comes on at 9:40 since the service is televised at 11:00. We have much larger coverage with WLWI AM. My devotional each morning is on WLWI AM and WLWI FM at 6:03.

See you at the "hugging" place Sunday!

— *John Ed*

April 28, 1985

WHY DO YOU GREET PEOPLE DURING WORSHIP?

Each Sunday morning during the Worship Service I ask every person to turn around and greet several people sitting around them. I know it doesn't look good on TV or sound good on radio, but it is important for people to meet the folks around them at worship. Everybody speaks to somebody and everyone is spoken to.

Early this month Bob and Mary Moorehead turned around and greeted people behind them. The man asked if Bob had any family in Ohio because he knew some Mooreheads. Bob explained that he had moved here from Ohio years ago. When Bob mentioned his father's name, it was the same name about whom the man was inquiring.

After the service of worship Bob continued the conversation and discovered that the visitors were Dick and Gloria Wymer who had just been transferred here from Ohio. They discovered that Gloria Wymer, was Bob's cousin. They had not seen each other in 40 years. Both of Gloria's parents had died when she was young and she went to live with another uncle. Forty years — and they sat down beside each other at the same service at Frazer Memorial United Methodist Church!

A few years ago a similar incident occurred. A young lady turned around and greeted the people behind her, and then I heard a shriek and saw two people hugging each other. This lady, about 30 years old, had met her grandmother for the first time. Her family had been involved in a divorce and she had moved with her mother out West and had never had the opportunity of meeting her father's parents. They were reunited at a service of worship at Frazer Memorial United Methodist Church!

Recently two couples greeted each other. They both were military and discovered that they had worshipped together at an Air Force Base in California years before and they both were now stationed here in Montgomery and were reunited at Frazer Memorial United Methodist Church!

See you at the "reuniting" place Sunday!

— John Ed

June 23, 1985

TRANSFER OF POWER

Last Saturday President Reagan took an unprecedented step in temporarily transferring power to Vice President Bush. Shortly before his surgery the President signed a letter directing Vice President Bush to temporarily assume the "powers and duties" of the Presidency while President Reagan was incapable of exercising authority himself. About 8 hours later he signed another letter reassuming his powers as President.

While there was a lot of controversy and confusion about this transfer of power, it seems to me that this is precisely what happens in our relationship to God. As long as we sense that we can make the right decisions of life, we want to keep the power to make decisions. When we come to that point in life where we realize that we are incapable, we transfer that function to God. This is what Paul meant when he said, "It is not I who lives, but Christ who lives in me."

One of the problems of life is that ours, like the President, is a temporary transfer of power. What God desires from us is a permanent transfer of power. God is not One on whom we call just when we get in trouble, or feel badly about situations, but One to whom we give a permanent transfer of power. That's what I will be preaching about this Sunday morning.

Even though the storms and rains came last Sunday night, it did not dampen the spirit of our Camp Meeting services. Sunday afternoon I was praying that it would not rain. Rolena Prescott and her fine committee had dipped over 1,000 scoops of ice cream and were wondering how they would keep them frozen. They were praying that it would rain! You know whose prayers were answered last Sunday night! We would have needed an ark rather than a flat-bed truck for the outdoor services!

But the rains and storms did not keep people from coming. We had over 700 present Sunday night. The spirit of the service was indescribable. I am grateful for a church family whose commitment is not based on what the weather does!

Four different families came up Sunday morning and introduced me to their new neighbors. They had just moved in and they were bringing them to church. This is the time of year people move to Montgomery. Check your neighborhood and invite somebody to come with you Sunday.

One visiting family came up to me and said, "This is the friendliest church we have ever seen. A stranger in the grocery store invited us to come, and everybody has made us feel at home. We have been invited to two different Sunday School Classes!"

See you at the "transfer of power" place Sunday! — *John Ed*

115

July 21, 1985

IDENTIFYING SIGNS

Our parking ushers do a super job each Sunday. They are here at 7 o'clock in the morning setting up the traffic cones to facilitate the flow of traffic. Their smiling faces and helpful directions assist you in parking your car. They are out there whether the temperature is 10 degrees or 100 degrees. We get so many favorable comments each week about them. Mike Maxey and his 50 volunteer parking ushers are a vital part of Frazer's ministry.

Recently the parking ushers shared that sometimes people forget where they park. They were trying to figure out some way to identify parking areas. One Sunday night one of the children was reciting the Fruit of the Spirit from Galatians 5:22-23. Someone suggested that the nine sections of the parking lots be identified by the nine fruits of the Spirit listed - Love, Joy, Peace, Patience, Kindness, Goodness, Faithfulness, Gentleness, and Self Control. Super idea!

When you park your car this Sunday, check the light post with the particular Fruit of the Spirit to help identify where you parked. If you have a special need in one of these areas of life, pick the section that you need help in and park there. One lady has already looked for "Long Suffering" because she wants to park her husband there! I insisted that we use the Living Bible translation of "Patience" rather than the King James version of "Long Suffering" because I could hear all of those comments linking "Long Suffering" with the sermons!

While the signs on the light posts will help you identify your parking area, it is far more important that the Fruit of the Spirit be identified in your actions each day. Parking in a particular area won't give you that aspect of the Fruit of the Spirit - opening your heart to God's will for your life and allowing Him to mold you in that area will make that aspect of the Fruit of the Spirit identifiable in your life!

This Sunday night we are privileged to have the Cameron Family sing. You have seen them on several national television programs. Philip Cameron is host of his own television program, "Connection," which is seen nationwide weekly. Invite a friend to come with you and share in a great service of worship.

See you at the "Identifying Signs" place Sunday!

— *John Ed*

August 11, 1985

116

LIFEGUARDS EVERYWHERE, BUT . . .

Last week 200 lifeguards with the New Orleans Recreation Department gathered at a city pool to celebrate the first summer in memory without a drowning at a New Orleans city pool. While they were celebrating at the pool, a 31-year old man, Jerome Moody, drowned in the very pool where they were celebrating.

Moody was not a lifeguard and was a guest at the party. He was fully dressed. It is not known when Moody got into the water or how he drowned. Some of the lifeguards pulled him out and tried to revive him until emergency medical attendants arrived. An autopsy confirmed that he had drowned.

It is so ironic that the 200 people were experienced lifeguards, and they were celebrating the fact that they had a trouble-free season. It was at that very pool that a man drowned.

It reminds me that we can gather quite often to celebrate what God is doing in our lives, and next to us there are people who are hurting and crying out for help - drowning. It doesn't matter how qualified a lifeguard is, he has to see the victim and respond to help before he drowns. Oftentimes it is easy for a church to celebrate some of the victories that God is claiming in the lives of people, and then overlook and fail to respond to persons right in our midst who are drowning.

People bring people to Christ and the church. Eighty-five percent of the people who come to Frazer and join come at the invitation of a friend. Most of those invitations are issued in the office, on the tennis court, in the grocery line, in the neighborhood, etc. Your natural web of contacts is the most logical place to start in witnessing for Christ and His church.

It is hard for me to believe that a man could drown in a pool with so many lifeguards standing around. I guess it is even harder to conceive how so many people in Montgomery are around "lifeguards" but never get invited to Life. Look around your neighborhood, your office, your natural webs of influence, - is there somebody to whom you need to reach out?

The effectiveness of lifeguards is measured by how well they guard lives - the effectiveness of a church is measured by how well it reaches people, disciples them, and sends them out to serve in Christ's name.

See you at the "lifeguard" place Sunday!

— *John Ed*

August 13, 1985

AN IMPORTANT MINISTRY

God uses so many different means to touch the lives of people. Some might think that a sports program in a church is purely recreational — I believe that it is a vital avenue that God can use to reach people.

This past summer Frazer fielded 10 softball teams in competition. Each of these teams represented the church well. This involved about 200 men and women in fellowship and competition. I received a letter last week from the wife of one of the ballplayers. I want to share a portion of it with you.

"This time last year I did not know anything about Frazer. My husband and I were not involved in church and did not have the Lord in our lives.

"We started attending Frazer last December because my husband was interested in playing softball. We could feel something very exciting every time we walked in the church, although the size of the congregation seemed scary at first. I can tell you first-hand that the Lord worked a miracle at our house through that team?

"Softball got us to Frazer, and Frazer got us to the Lord. The Lord knew how to get us to turn to Him and I am so glad that He did. Even though we have experienced a personal tragedy and a change in jobs, we have been happier in the last year than we have ever been because we know the Lord!"

This Sunday morning I would like to recognize all persons who were involved in the softball program. The various teams won about 15 big trophies of which we are proud but the most important victories came in the lives of those who participated. Right after the 11 o'clock worship service I would like to ask all persons who played softball to meet in the sanctuary for a group picture.

See you at the "ministry" place Sunday!

— *John Ed*

September 15, 1985

CHECK THE INVITATION

Two weeks ago several hundred fugitives in the Washington, D.C. area received an invitation to attend the pregame brunch and a Washington Redskins football game. Over 100 fugitives responded to the invitation and appeared at the D.C. Convention Center for the special brunch. The building was decorated with signs saying, "Let's Party" and "Let's all be there."

An added incentive in the invitation was that a new sports television station would be providing the free tickets. The invitation said that 10 of the lucky persons would receive 1986 Redskins season tickets and that a grand prize would be held for an all-expense paid trip to the Super Bowl XX in New Orleans.

Many of the fugitives showed up wearing bright burgundy and gold wool Redskin hats and Redskin buttons. The U.S. Marshals showed up disguised as cheerleaders, Santa Claus, and one marshal was dressed in a large yellow chicken suit with oversized red boots, while another turned up as an Indian Chief complete with large headdress. Other marshals were wearing tuxedos. When everyone got on the buses, they went to the police department's central cellblock instead of RFK Stadium.

The invitation was beautiful — the result was jail. The prisoners fell for it hook, line and sinker. U.S. Marshals called it the largest mass arrest of fugitives in recent history.

As you begin a New Year, check out your invitations carefully. So many times we are invited to something that looks so great — and it winds up as a trick. We become imprisoned by things that look so innocent in the beginning. The only invitation on which you can really depend in committing your life is the invitation of Jesus when he said, "Come follow me."

This is the last Sunday in the year and it is a Fifth Sunday. The choir will be singing a couple of my favorites, "Amazing Grace" and "I Go To The Rock." We are fortunate to have Joe and Sharon Pate sing. Both are professional musicians in New York City. Sharon is Bob Cooner's sister. They will be singing Sunday morning. Invite someone to attend with you.

See you at the "invitation" place Sunday!

— John Ed

FOR THE RECORD

On New Year's Eve in Rochester, New York, 54,500 people huddled around bonfires and played kazoos. They did this in order to break the previous record — a 40,000 kazoo chorus at a football game in Nashville in November — and thus go into the Guinness Book of World Records. The new record holders played "Take Me Out To the Ball Game."

Last weekend Christian coaches talked about going out to the ball game, but they weren't playing kazoos. They were interested in contributing to record books not in the win/loss column, but the column of influencing young people for Jesus Christ. So many of them stated that it was one of the finest experiences of their lives.

I reported for the record our church statistics for 1985. Every Methodist preacher has to do this. We received 774 new members, with 192 of these coming on profession of faith, to end the year with 4,412 members. This is a net gain of 553 which is probably the largest of any Methodist church in America.

Our Sunday School attendance average for 1985 was 1,528, which is an increase of over 200 for the past year. Our Morning Worship attendance average was 2,711, and our Evening Worship attendance average was 752. If I could have estimated, it would have been much better. That's actual count and it includes those bad weather and holiday Sundays. While I don't have access to the statistics of other churches — each of those probably will be right at the top, if not the top, of Methodist Churches in America.

The most exciting thing to me is the involvement of the people of Frazer. Most churches our size have up to 40 or 50 percent of the people inactive. We define inactive as missing 3 consecutive Sundays. Through the volunteering of the Frazer family to be involved in meaningful ministries, only 8 percent of the resident membership was inactive at the end of the year. It really doesn't matter how many members a church receives, the important factor is in the involvement and ministry outreach of the membership!

I am not nearly as interested in putting records in the Guinness Book of World Records as I am in leading people to have their names in the Lamb's Book of Life. Foolish records like playing kazoos will be replaced in the future — God's records will never be replaced or broken!!

See you at the "record" place Sunday! — *John Ed*

January 12, 1986

THE NAME OF THE GAME

Napolean McCallum was an All-American running back from the Naval Academy. He was recently selected as the most valuable player in the Senior Bowl in Mobile. While other great college players will be negotiating lucrative pro contracts in the next few months, McCallum will be going to Supply Officer's School in Athens, Georgia. He has made a 5-year commitment to serve in the Navy.

McCallum said, "I have an opportunity to serve — I feel good about it." He will not try to pull any strings to get out of that commitment to serve earlier. He said that it used to bother him about other athletes getting all that money — but, "Now I feel good about what I am doing. A lot of kids look up to me and that is very important to me."

That's a good kind of person to look up to — someone who wants to serve. Many of the Frazer family met McCallum when he was here for the Blue-Gray game and attended Worship at Frazer on Sunday. It is refreshing to see you a young man more interested in serving than in signing a lucrative contract.

The Russell Corporation in Alex City, Alabama is the only company that makes something that every National League Football team wears. The reason Russell has been successful in recent years while other apparel operations have suffered immensely is the fact that they major on service. Whichever team won the Super Bowl — that team would be wearing Russell garments. The reason — coaches and managers say, "The best thing about them is their service."

I enjoyed preaching last week about "The Seal of Being A Super Winner" through serving. This week I will be preaching about "The Spirit of Serving." Jean Costner, an outstanding soloist from Birmingham, will be singing. We will install Administrative Board members and commission every person who will be serving in various areas of the life of the Church.

Serving is the name of the game. It is more important than a big pro contract or looking for a place that will serve me. Jesus said, "If you try to save your life you will lose it, but if you lose your life in My service, you will find it."

See you at the "serving" place Sunday!

— John Ed

January 19, 1986

INTERPRETERS

One of the most interesting parts of my trip to Japan and Korea was the use of an interpreter every time I spoke. I was teaching pastors in Church Growth Seminars during the week and then preaching in local churches. I always used an interpreter. I would speak a sentence, and then it would be interpreted into their language.

I learned a lot about interpreters. Without an interpreter, I could not have communicated at all with the people. Somebody had to put into the native language of the people what I was trying to say. It occurred to me that this is part of the function of a Christian. God's message must be interpreted to the people for our culture by us. What God has to say to the world comes through the interpretation of people like you and me.

An interpreter never makes up the message, but simply relates what the speaker has said. We are not called to make up a message that today's world needs — that message has already been delivered through God's Word. We do not alter or change that Word, but we must interpret it into the language of today.

It is extremely important for an interpreter to be accurate. At one point I used a verse which says, *"He that hath the Son hath life."* The interpreter thought I said, *"He that hath the Son hath a wife."* That interpretation missed the whole point. One little letter in one word changed the whole meaning. It is very important for us to give careful attention to small details. A lot of times people are watching us, and how we react in little things in life carry a big message about our relationship to God.

An interpreter has to know both the language of the speaker and the language of the listener. He becomes the "go-between." I believe that's our task as Christians. We must bathe ourselves in God's Word, then we must be conversant with today's culture so that we might adequately interpret the message. God's Word is true and powerful, but until it is interpreted into the lives of the people with whom you work and live everyday, they may never hear it.

I loved preaching through an interpreter. I was fortunate to have good interpreters and they made the interpretations sound far better than the message I was trying to present. A few times I was even curious to see what they were interpreting! I hope you and I can make God's Word so exciting and appealing as we interpret it today.

See you at the "interpreting" place Sunday!   — *John Ed*
April 27, 1986

WORDCASTERS

Recently I read about a new concept in advertising/marketing that is being used out West. It is called "Wordcasters." It consists of about 1400 people in a target area who tell everybody they meet about a product for which they contract. It is person-to-person communication. This is proving to be more effective than television, radio, or newspaper.

I understand that the 1400 people are contacted by telephone and each of them is employed as a "Wordcaster." It is their responsibility to meet a lot of people and during a given period of time tell everyone about that product. The personal word motivates people more quickly than the mass media.

The Church is entrusted with the "best news" the world could possibly hear. There is no product on the market that can compare with the new life that is found through Jesus Christ. Every member of the church is a "Wordcaster!" Here at Frazer we can deploy over 4000 people to the target area of this city. If every member of Frazer shares his/her faith with several people each day — dream what would happen!

The personal word is always the most effective means of motivation. The most convincing witness is the one that comes from the heart of the person who has experienced that to which he gives a witness. That is convincing and contagious.

Person-to-person — that was the method that Jesus used. When you read the unfolding, exciting story in the book of Acts, it was "Wordcasting." People shared their faith with their neighbors.

I was in the Kwang Lim Methodist Church in Seoul, Korea, and they have 18,000 members. Six years ago they were about the same size of Frazer. The whole secret is that people are bringing people. The Bulletin insert for Sunday, April 10, listed the names of about 60 people who had joined the Church the previous Sunday. Beside each new member's name was the name of the person in the Church who brought them to Christ and the Church. They have already received 646 new members in 1986. Since that was a month ago they are probably over 800 by now! But the secret is people bringing people.

Meet with me Sunday as we make plans for Wordcasting next week. Some of our best Wordcasters are nurses and we will be honoring them on Nurse Appreciation Sunday.

See you at the "Wordcasting" place Sunday!   — *John Ed*

May 4, 1986

A NEW CONVENIENCE BUSINESS?

I heard on the radio last week about a funeral home in California that is constructing a new building featuring a large plate glass window and drive-through to display the dead bodies where viewers can simply drive through in their cars and stop and view the remains of the dead person. Viewing will be possible 24 hours a day. Supposedly there are a couple more of these in the United States.

The selling point is that it will make it convenient for people to come and view the remains without ever getting out of the car. I understand there is a button that you press and hear a tape recording of the obituary of the dead person. There will also be provided a place that you can sign so the family will know that you have driven through. It's so convenient you won't even have to dress appropriately to visit the funeral home.

I have never been much for wanting to view the remains of dead people. The most important thing about a person is not the body but the soul. What you view as the remains is not the real person. The shell that remains is unimportant compared to the soul that God created.

What I really like to view are the things that remain after the person has died — the footprints that they left on society. We have had some people to die recently in our church that have left a lot of remains behind — changed lives, role models, creative ideas, Sunday School lessons that have left a lasting impression, many deeds of love and kindness, etc. Those are the kind of remains the world needs to view, and they're not left conveniently.

Funerals are not for the dead person but for those who remain alive. At a time of death it is very important to go and visit with the remaining family. People often tell me they don't know what to say. What one says is not as important as the fact that one has gone to be with them. What the world needs is not a drive-through viewing, but genuine, compassionate presence with people. Folks won't remember what you say — they will always remember that you were there.

There is not a convenient way to die, and convenience is not what we look for at the time of death. Conveying strength and concern is far more important than convenience!

See you at the "non-convenient" place Sunday!

— John Ed

June 22, 1986

INOCULATIONS

Last Sunday afternoon at the church I saw a group of people laughing, having a good time and serving refreshments, so I went in. All of a sudden I discovered that I was in the inoculation party for all the people going on the medical trip to Kenya. They were taking their shots to inoculate them against cholera, typhoid, tetanus, and other diseases not common to Montgomery's environment.

Part of the ministry of the church is to help inoculate us against the things that we face each day that are not common to our spiritual health. The church's ministries are designed to encourage and promote good spiritual health. All that the church does is a process of that inoculation.

This Sunday we begin our Camp Meeting Month. Dress casually. Our Worship Services will be very informal. There will be a personal witness at each service. Joe Pat remembers those early Camp Meeting days in America and will select the kind of songs they used to sing! Our Evening Worship Services will be outdoors on the new property. Bring a chair or blanket to sit on. We'll provide a fan. Enjoy watermelon after the Worship Service. I'll be preaching at the Church in the Pines Sunday morning and will look forward to being here Sunday night.

During the month of June we received 70 new members which is not only more than we had received in any previous June, but more new members than any summer month in previous history! There are so many new people moving to the Montgomery area — invite someone to attend with you this Sunday. New growth provides great inoculation!

Vacation Bible School was the largest ever as we reached 830 during the week! We are gearing up for the largest Youth Work Project ever. Our Terrific Tuesdays for children is attracting more children than ever. At our first Older Adult program we expected about 50 and had over 100! Our Singles classes grow every week!

The group last Sunday reminded me that inoculations don't last forever — they have to be updated and renewed. The same is true of our spiritual inoculation process.

See you at the "inoculation" place Sunday.

— *John Ed*

July 6, 1986

THE IMPORTANCE OF PLANNING

Today the 40 top scientists in the U.S.A. are secluded in Building 29 on the neatly landscaped grounds of GA Technologies in LaJolla, California. They are planning for the future. They are called the Jasons, after the mythical Greek hero.

This group has met annually since 1960. At that time they were planning what we now call "Star Wars" lasers. A secrecy surrounds most of what they are doing. The building in which they work is regularly checked for bugging devices. They meet for about 5 weeks, and are paid $500 per day.

Our Long Range Planning Committee is not working secretly, is not being paid, but is trying to dream God's dream for Frazer's future. Our committee is called "The Joel Committee," because Joel encouraged the people to dream dreams and see God's vision.

The Joel Committee has accumulated a lot of statistical data. The area surrounding Frazer had 33,000 population in 1980. In 2005 the projected population is 113,000. Dr. Bill Clark has written a computer program which takes the growth of each age category in the church for the past 5 years and projects the expected average attendance of that class through the mid 1990's. An example is that we are averaging 240 babies per Sunday, and utilize 510 volunteers in 8 rooms in the nursery ministry. In 1991, we are projecting 350 babies per Sunday, utilizing 18 rooms and 900 volunteers. Similar projections are being made for each area of Frazer.

The Joel Committee is not working in secret — we are soliciting suggestions and information from every person. The planning process is a vital tool that God uses to bless the growth of His church. It is exciting to work with people who are prayerfully planning for God's future for His church.

The Jasons will be filing a report in late August. It will contain a lot of classified information for such agencies as the CIA and other government agencies. The Joel Committee's report will also be filed in late August, but there will be no classified information. It will be shared with the Administrative Board for their action and the entire Frazer family.

See you at the "planning" place Sunday.

— John Ed

August 10, 1986

TRANSPORTATION THAT TRANSPORTS

Last week I was driving along Highway 82 on my way to the Tygart Camp Meeting in Valdosta, Georgia. In the Eufaula and Albany areas I was fascinated by long lines of vacant boxcars sitting on the railroad tracks alongside Highway 82. There were miles and miles of empty boxcars. Many of them have weeds and kudzu growing over the sides of the boxcars.

The fascinating thing was the message on the side of the boxcars. One of the messages said, "Southern gives the green light to innovations." Obviously the innovations had failed somewhere because these boxcars appeared now to be obsolete. Instead of being on the "cutting edge" of new development in transportation, these boxcars are collecting kudzu through their inactivity.

On the side of each boxcar was also the message, "Southern serves the South." Now that's a good motto, but these boxcars did not look like they were serving very much. Instead of being actively involved in the transportation industry, they sit sadly sidelined with a good idea but not much to show as a result of it.

I have been told by some of my nonchurch friends that they view the church something like boxcars. Some church people put out all the right words and have all the right mottos, but what they are doing is inconsistent with what the church stands for. Most people in the church know the right answers — they just don't put them into practice.

In sharp contrast my mind raced to those "bullet trains" that I rode in Japan recently. They travel up to 150 mph and operate precisely on the minute. They didn't have any mottos or slogans on the side of them — they just transported people to their destination on time. Many of those "bullet trains" were so crowded that there was standing room only. I am told that they are efficient, dependable, and their track record for accidents is almost perfect. I pray that Frazer will be more like those "bullet trains" than those side-lined boxcars.

My friend, Albert Long, will be here to speak Sunday night and each night next week during our Youth Week. He is on the "cutting edge" of youth ministry. And the music with Mark Dickerson and Susan Langford will be super! Invite some young person to get on board — it starts at the Station Sunday. You won't find any kudzu collecting on the youth ministry at Frazer!

See you at the "transportation" place Sunday!   — *John Ed*
August 17, 1986

FAMILY REUNION

Chris White and Chris Yerby both are tall, dark haired, played basketball, and share the same name. A lot of people in Corpus Christi even told them that they walked alike. Recently they discovered that they are brothers — adopted by different families at birth!

Chris White's mother, Margaret, said "When I first saw Chris Yerby, I was spellbound. My instincts told me there was no doubt they were brothers." The boys were reunited last year at Carrol High School where they played basketball. They became friends and realized that their backgrounds were filled with coincidences.

As the Boys began to talk they discovered that they both were adopted and both were born in Austin. Their adopted parents began an 8 month search which last month traced their natural parents and confirmed their suspicions.

Chris Yerby said, "Knowing he is my brother makes things different. It is a deep feeling." They spent a September weekend together at Texas A & M for the first time after learning their family ties.

World Communion Sunday is a time for reunion when we affirm who our brothers really are. It highlights the fact that we have a common bond through the blood of Jesus Christ. We discover that there are people of other denominations and people of other nationalities around the world who share in our brotherhood.

This Sunday we join with millions of Christians around the world in celebrating the Lord's Supper on World Communion Day. Christians of all backgrounds and faiths join in a great reunion of brothers. Our World Communion Service will be televised and I invite people who cannot attend to have the elements of Holy Communion available so that they might participate in this reunion. I will lead the television congregation in a time together of receiving Holy Communion.

See you at the "reunion" place Sunday!

— John Ed

October 5, 1986

ABOUT THE AUTHOR

Dr. John Ed Mathison is the Senior Minister of the Frazer Memorial United Methodist Church in Montgomery, the fastest growing United Methodist Church in America. In 1986 the Church Leadership Institue cited Frazer as the fastest growing church for denomination in Alabama. The church has had a net gain of over 2,200 new members in the last five years.

Frazer has an average worship attendance for the 4 Sunday Services of 4,000. Part of the secret of growth has been the assimilation and involvement of people in meaningful ministries. Over 3,500 people are involved in specific areas of ministry. The church has set a goal of no more than 10 percent of the resident membership as inactive (anyone who misses 3 consecutive Sundays is considered inactive), and the church is presently staying within the goal. Frazer utilizes many part-time staff persons and secures most of its staff members from the local congregation.

In the book, *See How They Grow,* edited by Dr. Alan Walker and published in 1979, 12 growing churches throughout the world were selected as a subject for each chapter. The United Methodist Church selected was Frazer Memorial. Frazer Memorial was also featured in the movie, *Finding the Way Forward* produced by the Board of Discipleship of the United Methodist Church.

Dr. Mathison graduated from Opelika High School, attended Young Harris Junior College, received the B.A. Degree from Huntingdon College, B.D. Degree from Candler School of Theology, the Th.M Degree from Princeton University and the Doctor of Ministry Degree from Candler School of Theology.

In 1963 he traveled with the Venture for Victory Basketball Team through several countries in the Orient. The basketball team competed against the olympic teams and college teams in Oriental countries, and at half time presented a Christian witness. The team spoke to more than 20,000 people every day.

Dr. Mathison was an All-State Basketball Player for three years in high school and was captain and leading scorer for Huntingdon College. He has several times been ranked number one in his age division in tennis in Alabama and recently was ranked number three in the South. He has won six state racquetball championships.

For several years Dr. Mathison has served as Platform Speaker for the National Conference of Fellowship of Christian Athletes, and Platform Speaker for the National Hi-Y Tri Hi-Y Conference at Black Mountain, North Carolina. Twice he has been the Platform Speaker for the Protestant Retreat at the Air Force Academy at Colorado Springs.

He was selected as "Man of the Year" in Montgomery for 1978 and received the Distinguished Service Award from the Jaycees in 1979. He serves on the Board of Directors of Colonial Bank N.A., Board of Directors of the Montgomery YMCA, and the Governor's Council on Physical Fitness.

He is married to the former Joan Walters of Tuskegee, Alabama, and has one daughter, Vicki, 24 years old, and one son, Si, 20 years old.